Advanced Introduction to Comparative Constitutional Law

Elgar Advanced Introductions are stimulating and thoughtful introductions to major fields in the social sciences and law, expertly written by some of the world's leading scholars. Designed to be accessible yet rigorous, they offer concise and lucid surveys of the substantive and policy issues associated with discrete subject areas.

The aims of the series are two-fold: to pinpoint essential principles of a particular field, and to offer insights that stimulate critical thinking. By distilling the vast and often technical corpus of information on the subject into a concise and meaningful form, the books serve as accessible introductions for undergraduate and graduate students coming to the subject for the first time. Importantly, they also develop well-informed, nuanced critiques of the field that will challenge and extend the understanding of advanced students, scholars and policy-makers.

Titles in the series include:

International Political Economy
Benjamin J. Cohen

International Conflict and Security Law
Nigel D. White

The Austrian School of Economics
Randall G. Holcombe

Comparative Constitutional Law
Mark Tushnet

Advanced Introduction to

Comparative Constitutional Law

MARK TUSHNET

William Nelson Cromwell Professor of Law,
Harvard University, USA

Elgar Advanced Introductions

Edward Elgar
Cheltenham, UK • Northampton, MA, USA

Published by
Edward Elgar Publishing Limited
The Lypiatts
15 Lansdown Road
Cheltenham
Glos GL50 2JA
UK

Edward Elgar Publishing, Inc.
William Pratt House
9 Dewey Court
Northampton
Massachusetts 01060
USA

A catalogue record for this book
is available from the British Library

Library of Congress Control Number: 2013957776

ISBN 978 1 78100 731 0 (cased)
ISBN 978 1 78347 351 9 (paperback)
ISBN 978 1 78100 732 7 (eBook)

Typeset by Servis Filmsetting Ltd, Stockport, Cheshire
Printed and bound in Great Britain by T.J. International Ltd, Padstow

Contents

1   Introduction: comparative constitutional law – history and
    contours   1

2   Constitution-making   10
    2.1   Why make a constitution?   10
    2.2   The foundation of constitution-making: the
          constituent power   13
    2.3   The processes of constitution-making: questions
          about inclusiveness   19
    2.4   The substance of constitution-making: scope and
          comprehensiveness   24
    2.5   Why comply with the constitution?   36
    2.6   Conclusion   38

3   The structures of constitutional review and some
    implications for substantive constitutional law   40
    3.1   Introduction   40
    3.2   Establishing constitutional review   41
    3.3   Political constitutionalism as an alternative to
          constitutional review in the courts   44
    3.4   The classical issues in the structure of constitutional
          review   48
    3.5   New structures of constitutional review   56
    3.6   The relation between structures of constitutional
          review and second- and third-generation
          constitutional rights   63
    3.7   The structure of constitutional review and third-
          generation rights   67
    3.8   Conclusion   69

4   The structure of rights analysis: proportionality, rules and
    international law   70
    4.1   Introduction   70

4.2   Balancing, proportionality and rules compared   71
4.3   Explaining the difference   83
4.4   A different alternative to proportionality review   88
4.5   The role of international law in domestic
       constitutional law   91

5   The structure of government   94
5.1   The classical enumeration of the branches of
       government and its modification   94
5.2   An emerging fifth branch of government?   96
5.3   Beyond the fifth branch – or modifying the three-
       branch model   108
5.4   Conclusion   112

6   Conclusion   114
6.1   Forms of constitutionalism other than liberal
       constitutionalism   114
6.2   Constitutions for modern and highly divided nations:
       contradictory definitions of "thin" constitutions   116

References   122
Index   127

1 Introduction: comparative constitutional law – history and contours

Interest in comparative constitutional law has historically come in waves, typically triggered by dramatic examples of constitution-making – in the aftermath of the Second World War, in the era of decolonization and in the third wave of democratization that began with the displacement of Latin American dictatorships in the 1970s and continued through the breakdown of the Soviet Union and its satellites in Central and Eastern Europe (Fontana 2011).[1] During each wave a persistent set of issues arises about the boundaries of the field: How is it related to the study of comparative politics, for example, or what is its relation to normative theories of liberal constitutionalism?

Current interest in comparative constitutional law is a legacy of the third wave in the late twentieth century. The field appears to have become "self-sustaining", that is, not dependent upon triggering events. There is an International Association of Constitutional Law, with regular meetings drawing together scholars from around the world, as well as a leading journal, the *International Journal of Constitutional Law*, dedicated to comparative constitutional law. The decade of the 2010s has already seen the publication of three major research handbooks on comparative constitutional law, each conceiving of the field in slightly different terms (Ginsburg and Dixon 2011a; Rosenfeld and Sájo 2012; Tushnet, Fleiner and Saunders 2012).

The field has undergone relatively rapid evolution. Issues that were central to discussions in the 1990s, such as the comparative treatment of hate speech and sexually explicit materials, have fallen to the periphery, though scholars continue to examine some aspects of them. New issues have arisen. These include increasingly detailed and sophisticated analyses of the doctrine of proportionality and its

---

1 This is not to say that individual scholars have not struck out on their own, during periods when only a few scholars attended to comparative constitutional law. But, as a *field*, comparative constitutional law has been defined by triggering events.

alternatives,[2] and scholarship on the legal and conceptual status of procedurally regular constitutional amendments that courts nonetheless hold to be unconstitutional. Perhaps we can capture the shift as one from comparative study of the treatment of specific *topics* in domestic constitutions to the comparative study of general *themes* in constitutional law around the world.

The field of comparative law generally began to take shape in the late nineteenth century, driven in large part by processes of globalizing trade in a world of sovereign nations. For generations the idea propounded most eloquently by de Montesquieu – that each nation's laws reflected or embodied something distinctive about that nation's "spirit" or culture – dominated the thinking of legal scholars.[3] That idea counseled against the possibility of a field of *comparative* law, or at least a field of comparative *law* as distinct from, for example, anthropology or sociology that would identify a nation's "spirit" through an examination of its laws and then compare national "spirits". As trade globalized, however, legal actors in one nation necessarily had to learn about and deal with the laws of the nations with which they were transacting. The costs of international contracting (and, only slightly less so, the costs of the laws of tort/delict) pushed lawyers to develop methods of harmonizing apparently distinctive national laws. Harmonization could occur through the adoption of common statutory regimes – or through developing an understanding of the ways in which one nation's laws actually closely resembled those of another. The latter was the project of comparative law generally.

The economic forces that generated the field of comparative law were much weaker with respect to comparative constitutional law. Private law existed within a framework of public law, of course, but the details of any particular nation's public law rarely had much impact on the rules of private law with which economic actors had to deal. This was particularly true in an era of relatively low levels of administrative regulation of the economy. Even more, constitutional law was understood to be a fundamental, even defining, aspect of national sovereignty. The idea that one nation's constitutional law had much to do with another's – an idea that must somehow work its way into the field of comparative constitutional law – seemed incompatible with ideas

---

2 See, for example, Beatty 2004; Barak 2012; Bomhoff 2013.

3 Montesquieu himself was something of a generalizer, so what I refer to as a "Montesquiean tradition" might better be associated with Herder's romantic nationalism.

of sovereignty. The idea of harmonization (in the sense of conscious adoption of identical or closely similar rules), so important in the field of comparative private law, has played almost no role – even today – in comparative constitutional law.

It might also be worth noting that the first two waves of comparative constitutional law both occurred when issues of sovereignty were in some sense taken off the table. After the Second World War, for example, the allied occupation forces in Germany and Japan were key players in the development of those nation's constitutions. And in the era of decolonization, the colonial powers relinquished their sovereign control over their former colonies, which could then define for themselves their constitutional identities.

The field of comparative law arose in the nineteenth century when the idea that law could be studied scientifically was part of the orthodoxy of the legal academy in Europe and the United States. If Montesquieu and Herder can be associated with a tradition insisting on national distinctiveness, Bentham can be associated with the idea of functionalism as expressed in a universal grammar of government. To study constitutional law scientifically, scholars came to think, required the identification of functions common to all constitutional systems, such as the allocation of governing authority among the three branches of government that Montesquieu had identified – legislative, executive and judicial – or the protection of fundamental human rights (though it might be controversial which rights fell into the category). With the common functions identified, scholars could examine the different ways in which domestic constitutions performed those functions.

Yet the Montesquiean legacy persists in the field of comparative constitutional law. In its broadest version that legacy insists on the distinctiveness of domestic constitutional systems by emphasizing the ways in which domestic politics and domestic culture, broadly understood, determine how specific constitutional concepts are understood within each nation's legal system. A crude example might be the idea of electoral equality.[4] As is well known among political theorists, many quite different electoral systems can be defended as promoting one or another understanding of electoral equality: First-past-the-post systems embody one notion of electoral equality; list proportional representation systems another; and the alternative transferable vote yet

---

4 The example is drawn from Chryssogonos and Stratilatis 2012.

another. The Montesquiean perspective is that each nation's choice of an electoral system reflects that nation's understanding of what electoral equality requires, and that understanding is in turn developed out of the nation's politics and culture.

This formulation indicates an additional complexity in studying comparative constitutional law – its close connection to other disciplines and fields. A functional approach to questions about government structure, for example, almost inevitably points the scholar in the direction of comparative politics, where the determinants and effects of differences in structure are studied. Though political scientists and others who define their work as "comparative politics" tend to be inattentive to the details of any particular constitution, their studies do a great deal to illuminate questions about government structures.[5] Scholars of comparative constitutional law tend to focus on texts, and their interpretations, as well as the additional insights they can provide, beyond those developed by political scientists, may be rather small – at least with respect to government structures. Similarly, scholars of comparative politics have examined the implementation of constitutional provisions protecting human rights, again seeking to determine what leads to actual protection at varying levels.[6] And, again, a lawyer's focus on comparing texts and interpretations may have much less to offer than the political scientist's focus on implementation.

Another discipline related to comparative constitutional law is public international law and, particularly, international human rights law. Indeed, sometimes a reader is hard-pressed to distinguish between works that their authors identify as dealing with some aspects of rights in comparative constitutional law and works that the authors identify as dealing with international human rights law. *That* international law has penetrated domestic constitutional law is clear. *How* it has done so varies and that variation is a promising topic for systematic scholarly investigation.

Sometimes the connection between international law and domestic constitutional law is reasonably close. This is obviously true when international law is made part of domestic law by treaty and, where necessary, implementing legislation, with the effect of overriding domestic constitutional law. The constitutions of nations, including

---

5 See, for example, Persson and Tabellini 2003; Cheibub 2007.
6 See, for example, Epp 1998; Sikkink and Keck 1998.

South Africa, direct their courts to "consider" international law and authorize them to consider foreign law.[7] Interpretive practices in many other nations lead courts to do the same, without express authorization from the constitutional text.

Even where international law is not directly enforceable as such it might be incorporated into domestic law. The United Kingdom's Human Rights Act 1998 makes domestically applicable many of the rights protected in the European Convention on Human Rights. Argentina gives the Inter-American Convention on Human Rights status equal to other provisions in the nation's constitution. Some contend that the domestic constitution should be interpreted to give the jurisprudence of the Inter-American Court of Human Rights priority over the jurisprudence of the domestic courts with respect to domestic provisions. The question of the relation between supranational interpretations of international law and domestic constitutional law, where international law is not directly applicable, illustrates some of the complexities of the relation between international law and domestic constitutional law.

Many works in comparative law generally devote substantial attention to questions of method. Those questions arise in connection with comparative constitutional law as well, but have been addressed rather less. The reason may be that there is relatively little to say about methodology once the Montesquiean hurdles to paying attention to comparative constitutional law have been overcome. In any event, it may be helpful to identify some of the methodological issues in comparative constitutional law.

The first, unsurprisingly, is *language*. Domestic constitutional law is conducted in each nation's own language or languages. English and French are widely used. German is not, even though the German Federal Constitutional Court is one of the world's most important constitutional courts. Spanish is used in Spain and much of Latin America, but rarely elsewhere. Partly because of language issues, South and East Asia are relatively neglected areas of study. The Supreme Court of Malaysia issued an important decision on religious liberty in the *Lina Joy* case, but its opinion was written in Malay and there is no official translation into English, or even an officially endorsed translation by private law publishers.

---

7 See Constitution of South Africa, §§ 39 (1)(b) ("must consider international law"), 39 (1)(c) ("may consider foreign law").

The question of authorized translations is itself an important one. The official language of the Supreme Court of Israel is Hebrew, that of the German Constitutional Court is German. Both courts provide English translations of some of their decisions. However, the choice of which to translate is in each court's hands and a scholar has to be aware of the interests that might lie behind the selection of decisions to translate.

Deeper issues of language and translation arise in the Benthamite tradition of functionalism and universal grammar. The "natural" translation of some terms can be misleading. The term "judicial review" provides a good example even without translation. In US usage the term refers to the judicial practice of determining whether a statute is consistent with the Constitution; in British usage it refers to the judicial practice of determining whether administrative action is consistent with statutory authorization. The term used for the US practice is "constitutional review", a phrase largely unknown in US constitutional discourse.

Second, there are questions about the *units of comparison.* Traditionally, studies of comparative constitutional law offer comparisons among a handful of nations, sometimes only two, sometimes several located within a region. Methodologists have offered some criteria for choosing nations to study: Examining nations that are similar along many dimensions (the "least different" study) may help isolate specific reasons for distinctive treatment of individual topics, while examining nations that are quite dissimilar (the "most different" study) may help isolate some individual topics that are treated rather similarly in both, thereby, perhaps, pointing to some close-to-universal "requirements" for constitutional law (Hirschl 2005).

More recently, computerization has allowed the development of large data bases of national constitutions. Those data bases have begun to generate "large-N" studies, with accompanying statistical tests applied to identify the correlates and, perhaps, causes of variation among constitutions. Large-N studies in comparative constitutional law are at an early stage, largely because the data bases contain only basic information about constitutional texts – the number of discrete provisions, for example, or the existence of some sort of protection for free expression. The data are relatively thin, though. Consider one important study dealing with how long constitutions persist (Elkins, Ginsburg and Melton 2009). The authors must distinguish between constitutional amendments and constitutional replacement. But sometimes a constitution is dramatically transformed by an amendment, to the point where we might want to describe it as a "new" constitution. The United States Constitution furnishes an example. It is often described as the world's longest lasting constitution. Constitutional amendments adopted from 1865 to 1868, after the initial 1789 constitution proved unable to prevent an extremely costly civil war, changed the fundamentals of governance in the United States rather substantially – or so it can be argued. Should the United States be treated as having a single constitution from 1789 to the present, or two constitutions, one from 1789 to 1868, the other from 1868 to the present? Further, some scholars contend that the large expansion of national power during the Great Depression amounted to a constitutional amendment, or perhaps even a constitutional replacement. Data bases that merely enumerate constitutional provisions and the dates of their adoption will miss these nuances. Extremely careful coding might be able to address these issues, but at high costs of scholarly time and with the risk of limiting the utility of the data bases by transforming their "large-N" character into a mere listing of a large number of quite specific items.

Other equally difficult classification issues can arise as well. Consider constitutional protection for freedom of expression. Many European constitutional provisions protect freedom of expression in the first paragraph of one article then list permissible grounds for restricting that freedom in the next article. Other constitutions, such as Canada's Charter of Rights, have a general limitations clause applicable to all or most enumerated rights, including the right to freedom of expression. And the US Constitution protects freedom of speech without any listing of permissible grounds for restriction. A person preparing a data base of constitutions must at least engage in some quite careful coding decisions if the data base is to be useful for any but the most basic studies.[8]

Coding difficulties are likely to attend efforts to expand these data bases to include interpretations of texts as well as the texts themselves. Here the often-noted exceptionalism of the United States in protecting a right to bear arms provides a useful example. Elsewhere, constitutional courts have interpreted constitutional provisions about privacy or the right to the development of one's personality to create a constitutional right to self-defense against violent assault, and then found a right to possess weapons useful for self-defense entailed by those provisions – all without a text specifically protecting either the right to

---

8 For an example of the difficulties, see Ginsburg and Dixon 2011b.

self-defense or a right to bear arms.[9] It turns out that the United States, while something of an outlier, is not as exceptional as examination of constitutional texts might suggest. This could, of course, be detected through a large-N data base, but only if the coders were quite careful.

A final method used in comparative constitutional law might be called *illustrative* or *edifying*. Comparativists sometimes argue that comparative study can help dissipate a sense citizens have that only the constitutional provisions they are used to can possibly serve the nation's goals. (This is sometimes called the problem of "false necessity".) The Montesquiean tradition suggests that there might be some degree of necessity to a nation's laws, but that tradition was never completely deterministic: The national spirit might express itself in several ways, albeit perhaps within a restricted range. One might learn something about the possibilities available within one's own constitutional system by examining how other constitutional systems deal with roughly similar problems. Often this sort of comparative study is explicitly normative, recommending changes in domestic constitutional law by reference to other nation's constitutions.

Finally, it is essential to note that every approach to comparative constitutional law carries with it some ideological baggage. Most commonly today, the ideologies associated with the field are cosmopolitanism and liberal constitutionalism, countered only modestly by a positivism that sometimes works as a critique of the norms taken for granted by liberal assumptions associated with cosmopolitanism. For example, it is difficult to find scholarship defending restrictions on religious proselytization against the charge that they violate principles of religious liberty, on the ground that the restrictions serve an interest in preserving an aspect of national culture – but not at all difficult to find scholarship defending practices of minority communities against parallel charges, on the ground that preserving indigenous or minority cultures is consistent with liberal values.

In light of the complexities and potential scope of the field of comparative constitutional law, any introduction will inevitably reflect its author's interests. For example, large-N studies are treated only lightly in this book. And, importantly, the literature surveyed is almost entirely

---

9 See *Weapons Act Decision*, Supreme Court of Estonia, 11 October 2001, 8 East European Case Reporter of Constitutional Law 149 (2001) (holding that the right to possess a gun for hunting purposes was protected by the constitutional right to free self-realization).

written in English. With those qualifications, the chapters that follow do attempt to touch on a large number of questions that scholars of comparative constitutional law have addressed, but the emphases are my own.

2   Constitution-making

Alexander Hamilton's observation that the people of the thirteen colonies were the first to be given the opportunity to define their constitution "from reflection and choice" rather than "accident and force"[1] may have been accurate, but that opportunity now extends to people everywhere. The precise issues that constitution-makers confront vary widely and depend on the specific historical circumstances under which they operate. Generalizations are difficult, perhaps impossible, to come by. Yet, we can identify some issues about constitutional design that arise repeatedly. This chapter examines some of the more important conceptual and practical issues associated with modern constitution-making.[2] The conceptual and practical role played by the "constituent power" in constitution-making is a pervasive theme.

2.1   Why make a constitution?

Why make a constitution? Consider first a "new" nation, perhaps one that has successfully struggled to secede from another, or one that emerges from deep intra-national conflict. Such a nation might "need" a constitution for several reasons. The primary one is that in the modern world a constitution is probably regarded by the international community as a prerequisite to statehood, perhaps not as a matter of formal international law[3] but as a matter of practical reality. Second, and perhaps only the obverse of the preceding point, domestic actors may treat the existence of a constitution as establishing or symbolizing the nation's existence as a state. Third, constitutions are convenient ways of laying out the formal contours of the mechanisms for exercis-

---

1 The Federalist no. 1 (Hamilton).

2 The chapter touches on some issues about the content of modern constitutions, when such issues intersect with the topics of primary concern, but does not explore questions of content in detail.

3 Which may require not much more than effective control over a territory and, perhaps, some democratic means of governance, which need not, however, be instantiated by a constitution. *See* Montevideo Convention on Rights and Duties of States, art. 1 (1933).

ing public power. Finally, in nations with heterogeneous populations – an increasingly large proportion of the world's nations – a constitution can serve as an expression, perhaps the only one available, of national unity.

Constitutions as maps of power may be somewhat inaccurate. The realities of power may not be fully reflected in a constitution. For example, a nation's constitution might adopt a presidential form of government, yet the formal powers conferred on the president might not correspond to the practical power that the charismatic leader for which it was written actually has. Or the leader of the dominant party may hold a relatively minor public office yet be the effective locus of most important policy decisions. The inaccuracies can be even greater, as when constitutions purport to place limits on the exercise of public or private power in settings where that power is in practice unlimited. Standard usage is to describe constitutions where the inaccuracies are quite large as "sham" constitutions, with the so-called Stalin Constitution for the Soviet Union (1936) as the primary example. Yet the category of sham constitutions is inevitably imperfect. Practice in almost every nation will fail to correspond with some aspects of that nation's formal constitution, at least from some perspective, and so we need a metric for determining when the shortfall is great enough to make the constitution a sham. That metric is again almost inevitably going to be a matter of controversy: How much weight should it give to shortfalls with respect to rights as against shortfalls with respect to government structure, for example? Further, consider a nation where the shortfalls are unquestionably large. That nation's constitution might not be a sham if power-holders treat the constitution as aspirational, setting goals that they (sincerely) hope to achieve by pursuing the policies, concededly inconsistent with the formal constitution, they have adopted. This might suggest that the terminology describing some constitutions as "shams" is analytically important only because it helps us distinguish between shortfalls of varying degrees of severity, and helps us probe the plausibility of claims that any specific constitution is aspirational.

Constitution-making can occur in nations with established constitutions as well. Here we need to distinguish between amendments, which are routine,[4] and the replacement of a constitution in

---

4 At least conceptually, though the rules for placing amendments in the constitution may vary in their stringency. Stringent amendment rules of course reduce the rate at which amendments are successfully added to an existing constitution.

force.[5] Replacements can occur when the existing constitution has become outdated to the point where "merely" amending it would take a great deal of effort, particularly when specific desirable amendments might interact with existing arrangements in ways that require deliberate "reflection and choice". Or replacements can occur when those holding power under the existing constitution have become substantially discredited for reasons that critics associate with the constitution in place. These latter replacements might be described as involving constitution-making in crisis conditions, and so might be thought to resemble some post-conflict constitution-making processes. However, there are sometimes important differences between post-conflict and "discredited system" constitution-making.

Another form of constitution-making can be called "abusive" (Landau 2013). The idea of abusive constitutionalism is simple: Sometimes political leaders use the legal form of constitution-making to enact constitutional amendments or a new constitution with provisions that are inconsistent with constitutional*ism* understood in roughly liberal terms. The usual example is the accession of Adolf Hitler to the formal leadership of the German government, although the example is imperfect because the process that put Hitler in office was arguably unlawful.

Though the idea of abusive constitutionalism has some intuitive appeal, its analytic utility may be questioned. As an initial matter it is probably helpful to distinguish clearly between liberal constitutional*ism* and constitutional law, if only because every nation has a constitution – most written, some unwritten – but not every nation is a liberal democracy. Second and substantively similar to the difficulty of distinguishing between sham and aspirational constitutions, the category of abusive constitutionalism will have to distinguish between constitutions that contain some provisions that are inconsistent with some accounts of aspects of liberal constitutionalism, and constitutions that depart so substantially from liberal constitutionalism as to be abusive. This is likely to be particularly difficult when the constitution at issue is programmatic; that is, it sets out general policies the accomplishment of which is said to be constitutionally required. For some, aspects of a programmatic constitution are likely to be within reach only if the

---

5 As discussed below, the line between amendments and replacements is blurred in nations whose courts are committed to the doctrine that some amendments are substantively unconstitutional, and in nations whose courts enforce a distinction written into an existing constitution between constitutional amendments and constitutional replacements.

nation takes action inconsistent with some presuppositions of liberal constitutionalism.[6]

2.2 The foundation of constitution-making: the constituent power

In recent years the idea, originally articulated in the era of the French Revolution, that constitutions ultimately rest on a "constituent power", has returned to prominence in theorizing about constitutional fundamentals. Roughly speaking, the constituent power is the body of the people from whom the constitution's authority emanates. That rough statement conceals many complexities, however. The constituent power combines (1) something like a reference to real people whose consent is the basis of a constitution's legal legitimacy, with (2) the thought that a constitution's authority can derive from a collectively imagined project that no one fully holds and (3) a conceptual point about the *need* for something to serve as a basis for the constitution's authority.

One paradoxical way of identifying the core difficulty is this: The constituent power sometimes is called into being by the very process of constitution-making that presupposes the existence of the constituent power. Sometimes this is expressed in the proposition that constitution-making presupposes a *demos* – a people – for whom the constitution is to be a constitution (Weiler 1995). This appears not to be universally true, however. The United States may be an example of a nation that was created by the very act of constitution-making – whether that act occurred with the adoption of the Articles of Confederation or with the adoption of the US Constitution. And, more generally, sometimes constitution-making involves nation-*building*, the creation of a single nation unifying previously diverse entities. Perhaps the creation of the Federation of Malaysia out of various distinct Malay states, each under British control, is an example (Harding 2012). Constitutions created for the purpose of unifying a heterogeneous nation might be understood as vehicles for the creation of a *demos*.

---

6 Robert Nozick's famous argument against "patterned" accounts of distributive justice, accounts that are programmatic in the sense used here, was that such systems could not be sustained without interference with core liberal values (Nozick 1974). We need not agree with Nozick's general libertarian claims to see that there is something to his objection.

Normative and practical difficulties arise even when there is a pre-existing *demos* that can exercise the constituent power. Consider first post-conflict constitution-making, where the conflict has involved deep ethnic or religious divisions. The question of who constitutes the nation is likely to be at issue in the constitution-making process. This can have intensely practical aspects. Those participating in the process will have to decide from what territory the constitution-drafters will be drawn. Drawing the boundaries in one or another way will sometimes explicitly and almost always implicitly, determine who the *demos* is, in a setting where the parties implicated in the conflict all contend that they were part of all of the relevant *demos*. An example might be the creation and subsequent separation of India and Pakistan. Or consider that conflicts produce diasporas – people who once were unquestionably part of the *demos* and so, would have been included in the physically embodied constituent power, but who left the territory in part because of the conflict. Should those members of the diaspora who want to participate in the constitution-making process be allowed to do so?[7]

Further, the constitution-making body cannot actually be the people as a whole. For purely practical reasons that body can be at most representative of the people. Its members may claim to speak in the aggregate for the people, but shortfalls are inevitable. This is especially so where the constitution-making body is composed in substantial part of representatives of political groupings or "parties" – the scare quotes because the groupings need not have all or indeed any of the organizational trappings usually associated with political parties. Some groupings may be left out of the constitution-making process for seemingly practical reasons. They might be too small to warrant a seat at a table already crowded with representatives of larger groupings, or might lack the organizational capacity to participate meaningfully in the body's work. (Historically, of course, even large groups have been omitted from constitution-making – most notably, women. Today complete omission is rare, though under-representation is not.) Yet these small groupings might be socially or normatively significant, as with indigenous peoples in many nations. Even those who might claim to speak for the smaller groupings, such as representatives from non-governmental organizations (NGOs), sometimes have a problematic relation to those groups.

---

7 Improvements in international communications make it easier today to include the diaspora in these processes.

For these reasons it is perhaps misleading to think that the constituent power is an actual aggregate entity in the real world. Rather, it should be understood as a concept that helps explain the normative basis for a constitution's claim to authority. But, the difficulties and shortfalls sketched above raise questions about the nature of that claim to authority. The claim should probably be understood not as implicating something akin to sociological legitimacy, or the facts about whether or to what degree people actually believe themselves to be obliged to submit to authority, but rather in purely conceptual terms. The practical payoff, then, might be small, though using the idea of the constituent power does sometimes support clearer thinking about some practical problems.

A nation with a constituent power in the relevant sense must get the constitution-making process started somehow. Today, some constitution-making processes are assisted by elements of the international community, either international organizations, such as the United Nations, or individual nations (for a skeptical discussion, see Tushnet 2008). The assistance is provided when there is some need. Ordinarily, that need arises from within the nation. So processes with international assistance – or even prodding – ordinarily get started from within.

They do so, in general, in two settings. The constitution in place may provide mechanisms for its own replacement and the constitution-makers may use those mechanisms. But, to the extent that the constitution-makers are (or see themselves as) representatives of the constituent power, they may believe that they are not *legally* constrained by existing mechanisms. The theory is that those mechanisms are themselves the product of the constituent power, which always has unconstrained power. This is sometimes put in this way: After the constituent power creates a constitution, every action taken within that constitutional framework is an exercise of constituted power. This is clearly so, in this theory, of ordinary legislation, of ordinary constitutional amendments and even of constitutional replacements made according to the provisions of the constitution. But the constituent power always retains the power to re-constitute the constitution on its own terms, that is, on terms set at any time by the constituent power as it is. (International law might impose some constraints on the constitution-making process. For a discussion, see Widner and Contiades 2012.) So, for example, it is commonplace to observe that the US Articles of Confederation provided that they could be amended only with the unanimous consent of the states making up the Confederation, but the US Constitution – a replacement of the Articles – provided that the amendment would take effect when nine of the thirteen states ratified it. According to the theory of the constituent power, the example illustrates the constituent power being exercised in 1787–1789 in a manner inconsistent with the constituted power in the Articles, a constituted power that itself was an exercise of the constituent power in 1777–1781. Put another way, the constituent power always has the ability to call itself into being, disregarding restraints created *by itself* in an earlier appearance.

In a second version, constitution-making processes get started without there being a pre-existing framework for constitutional revision, which can be described as constitution-making in a vacuum. Twentieth century experiences of decolonization are good examples: Colonizing powers simply withdrew, sometimes facilitating the constitution-making process but not acting as participants in that process. Some revolutionary transformations are similar in structure. The *ancien regime* has collapsed and its supporters have fled, leaving the field open for a complete constitutional revision. As the term *ancien regime* suggests, revolutionary France can be taken as an example of this process and the flight of loyalists from the, to-be, United States gave the drafting of the US Constitution something of the same flavor.

France and the United States are imperfect examples of constitution-making in a vacuum and indeed, there may be no perfect ones. The reason is that constitution-making does not occur on a desert island to which the constitution-makers have just arrived. It occurs in real historical time under real historical circumstances. This leads to another tension in constitution-making exercises. The tension is between the power relationships as they exist when a new constitution is created and the power relationships that the new constitution both ratifies to some extent and creates to some extent.

Sometimes the collapse of the *ancien regime* means that its supporters have lost *all* political power. This may be true, for example, in some cases of imposed constitutions, where a conquering power creates a constitution for its now-defeated enemy. Nazis had no role in creating (west) Germany's Basic Law, for example. Still, the complete collapse of pre-existing political power is rare. Conservative supporters of the Japanese emperor played some part in the adoption of the post-war Japanese constitution even though it is usually described as a constitution imposed by the occupying forces (Soichi and Moore 1997).

Royalists were active participants in the French constituent assembly of 1789–1791 and even in Germany, conservative representatives participated in the Basic Law's creation.

More commonly, elements of the former regime participate directly in constitution-making. This is obviously true when the push for a new constitution comes when the existing constitution is understood to be functioning clumsily and so requires extensive but not revolutionary updating. More dramatic changes can occur only with the agreement or at least acquiescence of those empowered by the about-to-be-replaced constitution. Roundtable negotiations have become one important form of constitution-drafting. These negotiations bring together representatives of the regime in place with representatives of the forces that all acknowledge will soon take power. Communist parties sat at the negotiating table in Central and Eastern Europe as their political domination was disappearing, as did the white National Party in South Africa's roundtable negotiations.

The reasons for such participation are clear. Those dominating the existing regime are universally understood to be on their way out, but roundtable negotiations are aimed at smoothing the path to their exit. This means that the constitution being drafted has to gain their agreement. Otherwise they will resist being displaced and violence will break out (or break out again, in some cases). Even more, in many cases participants in the constitution-making process understand that those who formerly held complete political power will retain significant power after the transition. South African whites represented by the National Party would have substantial economic power in an African-dominated government and Communist parties in Central and Eastern Europe continued to have members who held on to strong collectivist visions of governance. So agreement from representatives of the former regime is needed not only to ensure a peaceful transition, but also to ensure that the new constitutional system is stable because everyone, including those representatives, finds it acceptable.

Constitution-makers hope that the institutions they are creating will be stable over time.[8] Political stability requires at least acquiescence from nearly all groups that have significant power, whether political,

---

8 This is true even of constitutions expressly understood as transitional, because the drafters of such constitutions typically envision in rough outline the contours of the regime that a new, permanent constitution will have. This is exemplified by the inclusion in the transitional South African

cultural, or economic. ("Nearly all" because on rare occasions it may be possible to create a constitution over the objection of a protesting minority, whose continuing protests will be met with forcible suppression by the new regime.) This requirement implies that even transformational constitutions project existing power relationships into the future, though they also seek to alter those relationships. Yet doing so poses risks. The projecting of power relationships may limit the achievement of transformative goals. Excluding representatives of the *ancien regime* from constitution-making processes – as occurred, for example, as a result of the military occupation of the defeated Southern states after the US Civil War – may generate resistance to the new arrangements, resistance that can itself limit the transformative possibilities.

We can bring out the tension that this exposes by overstating it as a paradox: Constitution-making processes will either be unnecessary or ineffective. Those holding power must agree to the new arrangements. But, they will do so only when they are confident that they will not be seriously disadvantaged by those arrangements. They can have that confidence when the new constitution does not change things much.

Clearly this is an overstatement. The post-communist constitutions and the South African Constitution did change things substantially, with the agreement of representatives of the former regimes who knew that their political positions would be significantly different once the new constitutions were in place. Some participants in constitution-making may understand, if only vaguely, that the new arrangements they are creating will start a process of incremental change in power that will build on itself to produce substantial alterations in the distribution of power over time. The intervening period may be long enough, or may be hoped to be long enough, for those benefiting from the existing distribution of power to adjust, leave, or learn how to regain power under the new arrangements. Still, it may be worth considering the possibility that new constitutions themselves do not change anything but only ratify a change in the distribution of power that has already occurred.

Jon Elster provides some support for the tension between effectiveness and irrelevance in his observation that constitution-making often

---

constitution of a set of principles that would have to be incorporated in, or provide the structure for, the permanent constitution. Interim Constitution of South Africa (1994), schedule 4.

occurs under circumstances unfavorable for careful design (Elster 1995). When constitution-making occurs during crisis or, sometimes, after the exhaustion of conflict, constitution-makers may find themselves pressed to reach some conclusion within a compressed time period.[9] The felt urgency conduces to quick compromises without substantial attention being paid to how the constitution will operate once adopted. Such constitutions may be ineffective. Where constitution-making occurs in the absence of a crisis, constitution-makers may deliberate carefully, but, feeling no real pressure, may largely re-inscribe in the new constitution the power arrangements of the existing one.

2.3 The processes of constitution-making: questions about inclusiveness

The US Constitution was drafted by an unrepresentative small group meeting behind closed doors. Such a process would generally speaking be unacceptable today. International organizations and NGOs would assert with some plausibility that it would be inconsistent with some soft norms of international law. It is almost certainly inconsistent with what specialists in constitution-making regard as best practices. Probably more important, except under unusual circumstances domestic audiences would regard it as an inadequate basis for generating a constitution that will become binding domestic law.

Contemporary constitution-making processes must be inclusive in some general sense. Satisfying that requirement at both the drafting and the adoption stages raises some interesting general questions.

2.3.1 Inclusiveness in drafting

Until recently it would have been obvious that constitution-drafting could not directly include wide segments of a nation's people. The only possibility was achieving inclusiveness by ensuring that the drafting body was sufficiently representative of all the relevant constituencies. Iceland's recent constitution-drafting exercise suggests that this might no longer be true in its strongest form. The drafting there was "crowd-sourced", with every Icelander having the right – and power

---

9 Sometimes the period may be extended over time, but then primarily because the parties to the negotiation treat the constitution-making process as a continuation of the crisis or conflict.

– to submit suggestions for constitutional provisions through a website maintained by the constitution-revision body. In that sense the drafting process included every Icelander who was interested in participating. One can imagine similar crowd-sourced drafting processes even for nations larger than Iceland. Existing political groupings and parties will almost certainly affect how crowd-sourcing and similar mechanisms of direct public participation in drafting actually operate. For example, parties may prompt their members to submit identical proposals, thereby multiplying the apparent public support for the proposals.

Of course the proposed Icelandic constitution was not "drafted" through crowd-sourcing, which generated ideas and tapped public sentiment. Someone had to do something with the citizenry's suggestions. Winnowing the outlandish from the strange but plausible, for example, would seem essential to making the process work. And, even were the drafters to start out regarding themselves as no more than charged with selecting the most popular suggestions and placing them in the constitution, they could not maintain that posture permanently. Some suggestions might be completely inconsistent with others. The drafters might submit them in the alternative to the public at the adoption stage. More important, constitutional provisions often interact. Suppose there is overwhelming support for Provision A, quite a bit of support for Provision B and slightly less support (but still a substantial amount) for Provision C. A constitution that contained A and B might be unworkable in predictable ways, so the constitution's writers might choose to place A and C in the constitution.[10]

The crowd-sourcing example illustrates a more general point about constitution-writing. An inclusive process can generate a wide range of perfectly decent proposals for the constitution, but integrating them into a single document that will serve as the blueprint for an effectively functioning government requires a fair degree of technical skill. The technicians, almost certainly lawyers and legal academics sometimes with the assistance of international organizations and NGOs, may regard themselves as faithful servants of the inclusive process. Almost inevitably, however, lawyers' technical concerns will have some effects

---

10 The best recent example of this kind of unworkability is Israel's short-lived experiment of electing a prime minister separately from electing parliament. Predictably, the prime minister lacked support from the parliament because voters chose a "leader" as prime minister and voted for narrower parties pursuing sectoral interests when they cast their votes for parliament.

– predictable and unpredictable – on the meaning of the constitution they write. To the extent that constitutions as written are to be *legal* documents, inclusiveness will be tempered to some degree by the necessary concern for technicality.

Inclusiveness will almost always be tempered by more than that, however. Assume that the drafting body – a constituent assembly – is adequately representative of the nation's constituents. Under modern conditions it will have to function with some substantial degree of openness. The secrecy of the US constitutional convention would no longer be broadly acceptable. As Jon Elster has emphasized, conducting constitution-writing in secret has advantages (Elster 1995). It allows participants to make unprincipled bargains, tradeoffs that cannot be justified on the basis of any deep view of what the new government should look like or do but are justified only on the shallow but important ground that the tradeoffs are required to get overall agreement on the constitution. Afterwards, the constitution's advocates can invent principled accounts to justify the results (not the tradeoffs), or hope that they will be ignored as part of a larger discussion. Furthermore, Elster argues, drafting in public leads participants to posture for public consumption and to stick with their positions longer than is desirable, out of concern for seeming to waffle on important issues.

As a practical matter, drafting can rarely be done in public anyway. Public discussions by drafters might produce agreement on a few items, but many others are likely to be intractable without hard bargaining of the sort that is difficult to do in public. Instead, the drafters will retreat to the back rooms, or to dinner tables, where the important work will be done. Whether a combination of seeming openness, or openness with respect to some matters with secrecy with respect to others, will be acceptable to modern audiences is probably highly dependent on circumstances. Some political cultures may accept the combination, others resist it. In the latter case and sometimes in the former, secrecy may be impossible for another reason: leaks. Again, unlike the conditions in 1789 Philadelphia, keeping sensitive information under complete control today may be close to impossible. A person angry about what has just happened behind closed doors may Tweet some information; some participant in the dinner table conversation may strategically disclose it "in confidence" to a journalist; many other variants are possible.

The effects of all this can be put as a chain of contradictions. Contemporary constitution-writing must occur in substantial part before an observing public, but effective constitution-writing must occur in substantial part behind closed doors, but keeping information behind closed doors is in practice impossible. Probably the best one can hope for is that sometimes things will work out so that there is "enough" openness and "enough" secrecy.

2.3.2   Inclusiveness in adoption

A newly drafted constitution must be adopted. And, again, today adoption generally requires a substantial amount of popular participation. Popular participation can take place at two stages after a new constitution is proposed – through processes that allow the people to propose and the constitution-drafters to adopt, revisions in the initial proposal and through ratification processes.

Both stages require the proposal's dissemination and dissemination cannot be merely mechanical – simply distributing the proposal widely. Rather, the nation's people must have the opportunity to understand the proposal. Technical and political issues can arise in connection with the educational processes necessary for effective dissemination. Particularly in nations with low literacy rates, the mechanisms for dissemination must use channels other than descriptive writing. In the recent past visual depictions in graphic form ("comic books", disparagingly) and radio and television transmissions were used; today social media are available. Using any of these alternatives raises questions beyond the technical, because translating the proposed written constitution into some other form inevitably alters its meaning. Some alterations will be substantively consequential, which means that those charged with the task of translation have the power to redefine some constitutional provisions, sometimes in politically controversial ways. Those who find themselves disadvantaged by the translation may organize to oppose going forward with the constitutional process; they may argue that they do not oppose the constitution as written, but rather the constitution as it is being described by the means of dissemination.

Even before the availability of crowd-sourcing techniques, sometimes the people can be asked to comment on the proposed constitution before they are asked to ratify it. Sometimes quite a substantial number of comments have been submitted. One can be skeptical about the value of the comment process. As with other forms of crowd-sourcing, popular suggestions may impair the technical integrity of the constitutional draft. More important perhaps, such suggestions run the risk of undoing compromises reached during the drafting process. Further, political groupings or parties that only grudgingly accepted the constitutional draft may use the comment process as a wedge for reopening matters that others regarded as settled. Popular participation may in this way undermine the very legitimacy that it is supposed to generate.

One response to these difficulties is to de-fang the comment process by treating it as merely cosmetic. That is, innocuous suggestions may be incorporated in a revised proposal to demonstrate that the comment process was meaningful, but truly significant suggestions, even those with substantial support, may be disregarded. More study of comment processes is needed, but it may well be that comment processes are more often cosmetic than substantial.

Either in its initial or a possibly revised form, a proposed constitution must then be ratified to become binding law. At this point the distinction between constitution-making via established amendment processes and constitution-making via some other mechanism returns to prominence. Depending on the existing constitution's amendment rules, new constitutions developed as constitutional amendments might not require popular ratification. So, for example, if the amendment rule requires only parliamentary approval by a qualified majority (such as a supermajority, or majorities in successive sessions), a new constitution adopted through the amendment process might not be submitted to the people for ratification. There might be an emerging soft norm of international law that requires popular ratification no matter what domestic mechanism for proposing a new constitution is adopted, though as a soft law norm the requirement lacks effective enforcement. Popular ratification is almost certainly regarded as "best practice" in constitution-making today.

Ratification is desirable, even if not required, in part to ensure that the new constitution has domestic legitimacy. Typically, ratification occurs through a national referendum. Some issues already mentioned recur at the ratification stage, but sometimes in a more focused way. Political parties may organize in support of or against ratification and their campaigns can have all the characteristics of ordinary political campaigns, including severe simplification of complex issues, sometimes to the point of distortion or deception. As with the general issue of constitutional replacement, so too must ratification address the concerns of those continuing to hold significant political power. So, for example, the Icelandic crowd-sourced constitution appears to have been de-railed by the unwillingness of politicians to accept some of its major innovations.

The ratification referendum may result in the adoption or defeat of the proposed constitution. Often, ratification defeats are described as failures, though the term may be inapt. A defeat may signal that the proposed constitution was not in fact well suited to the nation as it then was, even though it might be well-designed for a nation that might have been transformed were the constitution to have been adopted. In parallel, a referendum vote in favor of adopting the constitution should not in itself be treated as a success full stop. Whether it is a success will depend on how well the constitution functions once it has been in place and operating for a while.

2.3.3   Concluding thoughts about inclusiveness

The practical concerns about drafting and adoption show that the concept of constituent power intersects with practical issues of constitution-making. When Abbé Sieyès introduced the idea of constituent power, it served primarily a conceptual end, that of explaining why a constitution created as the French Constitution was created had a claim to authority: It had authority because it was an act of the constituent power convened in a self-described constituent assembly. Whether the participants in the constituent assembly actually represented real constituencies rather than notional ones was largely irrelevant. Today, real representativeness in its creation is the foundation of a constitution's authority. Inclusiveness is the contemporary mechanism for ensuring that a constitution actually is an exercise of the constituent power.

2.4   The substance of constitution-making: scope and comprehensiveness

This chapter is not concerned with the choice between having a parliamentary system or a presidential one, for example, or with the precise form constitution-makers give to processes for constitutional review of legislation (as to which see Chapter 3). However, we can examine some general issues of substance by moving to a higher level of generality.

2.4.1   Expressing foundational principles in a constitution

Often the hard work in constitution-making involves working out details of government structures, because different structures have different and to some degree predictable political consequences. Modern constitutions typically have preambles and other provisions stating general principles. Constitution-writers can and sometimes do omit preambles without sacrificing much. Most preambles combine pabulum – in references to general ideas about human rights, for example – with some effort to capture a sense of national identity. Most often, this combination serves some broad expressive or educational purpose, but occasionally more emerges from the preambles and general statements of principle.

Often these provisions are largely precatory, with relatively little legal effect. Legislators can rely on them, arguing that their proposals if adopted will advance the general principles or the aims articulated in a preamble. Often they are expressions of the constitution-writers' understanding of national identity. Sometimes, however, preambles and general principles can have practical and legal force. Occasionally, the expressive, practical, or legal effects of statements of general principles and preambles may create unanticipated difficulties for an operating constitution.

Preambles come in many variants. Some, like the US Constitution's, are terse and consist almost entirely of statements of general principle. Preambles consisting primarily of general principles are almost entirely forward-looking. More typically, preambles are both backward- and forward-looking.[11] They describe the nation's historical origins and the reasons for adopting this constitution. Post-conflict constitutions may refer to the struggle's resolution by the process resulting in the constitution being offered for adoption. Examples include the preambles to the 1937 Irish Constitution and the 1996 South African Constitution. The former refers to "centuries of trial" and the "heroic and unremitting struggle to regain the rightful independence of our Nation". The latter says that "the people of South Africa recognise the injustices of our past [and] [h]onour those who have suffered for justice and freedom in our land". Some preambles are long and quite detailed.[12]

---

11   Constitutions written to replace ones that have become outdated may simply pick up the preamble from the existing constitution.

12   See Preamble, Constitution of Hungary (2012).

The longer the preamble, the more likely it is to reflect the kinds of negotiated compromises that pervade constitutional details. The Iraqi preamble, for example, carefully includes as many of the peoples of Iraq as possible, so as to avoid the implication that one group has constitutional priority.[13]

Preambles can conceal as well as reveal important issues. Referring to a nation's "people" may, in specific contexts, signal to insiders and sometimes to others an ethno-nationalist understanding, for example. More generally, backward-looking statements may come to have exclusionary implications as a nation's population changes (Tushnet 2012). In the twenty-first century many nations are "nations of immigration", with increasingly large portions of their populations drawn from other lands (sometimes recently, sometimes over extended periods of time, as with the Turkish-origin population of Germany). Backward-looking statements may impede the development of a national self-understanding that comports with the nation's actual composition, and may even serve as the focal point for the creation or at least intensification of ethno-nationalist politics.

Even forward-looking statements of principle may have similar effects. Consider the terse "whereas" clause that precedes Canada's Charter of Rights and Freedoms: "Whereas Canada is founded upon principles that recognize the supremacy of God and the rule of law".[14] The reference to God may come to seem inapt over time. Similarly with the Irish Constitution's preamble, which expressly speaks "in the name of the Most Holy Trinity, from Whom is all authority and to Whom, as our final end, all actions both of men and States must be referred", and invokes principles of "Prudence, Justice and Charity", terms that resonate strongly with the natural law tradition. The weaker the ties of the people of Ireland (including immigrants) to the Roman Catholic Church, the more distance there will be between the preamble and the nation for whom it purports to speak. Focusing less on the terms as used in their historical context than on the general principles they articulate can alleviate these difficulties. Notably, the Canadian clause does not say that Canada is founded upon the supremacy of God, but rather on "principles that recognize" that supremacy. An atheist might

---

13 Preamble, Constitution of Iraq (2012) (invoking "the pains of sectarian oppression inflicted by the autocratic clique and inspired by the tragedies of Iraq's martyrs, Shiite and Sunni, Arabs and Kurds and Turkmen and from all the other components of the people").

14 This perambulatory clause is not labeled a preamble.

agree with the founding principles without agreeing that only God's supremacy justifies them.

Political theorists have raised questions about the motivational adequacy of purely principled, forward-looking statements of national identity. Their concern is that everyone in the world could agree with some such statements, which means that no one in the world will actually care about doing so. Who could disagree that the nation should promote justice and who will care much about whether some specific policy does so pursuant to a preamble rather than for justice's sake? Preambles that combine backward-looking statements about a nation's origins in struggle, with forward-looking ones about its ongoing commitments may provide a blend that can motivate loyalty to the constitution, though at some cost of being potentially exclusionary with respect to phrases evoking a past that not all citizens can plausibly say they share.

Preambles and general principles can have legal force when they are embedded in constitutions with provisions for constitutional review in the courts. Sometimes courts will rely on preambles and general principles as the grounds for specific exercises of the power of constitutional review. In France, the Constitutional Council's foundational decision on associations in 1971 referred to the preamble of the 1958 Constitution as stating some of the "fundamental principles recognized by the laws of the Republic", which provided the foundation for the Council finding a statute unconstitutional. The High Court of Australia invoked the general principle of representative democracy that underlay that nation's structures of governance to infer a principle of freedom of political expression even though the authors of the Australian Constitution deliberately refrained from including in it a comprehensive bill of rights, including a protection for free speech.[15] The US constitutional scholar Charles Black advocated for a method of constitutional interpretation that called on judges to make similar structural inferences from general terms and principles (Black 1969).

Constitution-writers might sometimes welcome structural constitutional interpretation. Even if constitution-writers hope to prevent it, they may find it difficult to express that hope in words that effectively constrain the technique. The authors of India's 1947 Constitution adopted a formulation used in Ireland's Constitution

---

15 *Australian Capital Television v. Commonwealth* (1992) 177 CLR 106.

to give constitutional status to social and economic rights. The Irish Constitution protected those rights through "directive principles of social policy", which were to be "the care of the [Parliament] exclusively and shall not be cognisable by any Court". The Indian Constitution changed the descriptive wording slightly, to "directive principles of state policy" and omitted the ban on judicial enforcement. That ban was generally understood as implicit in the constitutional structure, through an understanding confirmed by other constitutional provisions; the constitution distinguished between "fundamental rights", contained in Part III, which were enforceable in court, and the directive principles in Part IV. One could readily infer that they would not be enforceable in that way. Nonetheless, the Supreme Court of India has read into the judicially enforceable right to life many important social and economic rights laid out in the directive principles.[16]

2.4.2   Unamendability

Some constitutions single out specific substantive provisions and purport to make them unamendable (Ronzai 2013). The classic expression is the so-called "eternity" clause of the German Basic Law. That clause, Article 79, says that amendments "affecting the division of the Federation into [States] . . . or the principles laid down in Articles 1 and 20 shall be inadmissible". Article 1 states: "Human dignity shall be inviolable" and Article 20 describes Germany as "a democratic and social federal state". Article 20 also backs up these provisions: "All Germans shall have the right to resist any person seeking to abolish this constitutional order, if no other remedy is available." Some constitutional courts have followed the Supreme Court of India in articulating a doctrine according to which some constitutional amendments are substantively unconstitutional if they conflict with what that court calls the constitution's "basic structure" (Krishnaswamy 2009). Depending on domestic constitutional conditions and traditions, the basic structure can include both broad principles, such as federalism and secularism, or seemingly narrow provisions, such as term-limits for the nation's president.

Reconciling the proposition that constitutional provisions can be unconstitutional with the idea that constitutions are exercises of the constituent power is difficult. Suppose that the purportedly unconstitutional amendment is adopted by the amendment rules specified in

---

16 The foundational case is *Olga Tellis v. Bombay Municipal Corp.* [1985] 2 Supp SCR 51.

the existing constitution.[17] The amendment is an exercise of (a form of) the constituent power at the time the amendment occurs. It is unclear as a matter of basic theory why an exercise of the constituent power at an earlier time should prevail over an exercise of the constituent power – of a people constituted differently – at a later time.

The notion of "inadmissibility" might be thought to offer a solution. An amendment seeking to change an unamendable provision could be inadmissible in the sense that its proponents could not lawfully use the existing amendment procedure to get it adopted: Relevant officials might rule the amendment out of order, or refuse to place it on the ballot and, were courts called upon and agreed with the officials' judgments about substantive unconstitutionality, the courts would uphold such refusal. Sometimes the idea of an amendment's substantive unconstitutionality is coupled with the acknowledgment that the "amendment" could be adopted as part of a process of replacing the existing constitution with another – at least where the existing constitution itself lays out processes for constitutional replacement.

At this point the theory of constituent power comes in with real bite. Consider here the constitutional theory expressed in the US Declaration of Independence:

> [W]henever any Form of Government becomes destructive . . . , it is the Right of the People to alter or to abolish it, and to institute new Government, laying its foundation on such principles and organizing its powers in such form, as to them shall seem most likely to effect their Safety and Happiness. . . . [I]t is their right, it is their duty, to throw off such Government, and to provide new Guards for their future security.

Behind every constitutional structure lies the possibility of revolutionary overthrow – peasants with pitchforks, so to speak. The constituent power can exercise itself through the forms of law, but those forms cannot ultimately constrain the constituent power.

Inadmissible or unconstitutional constitutional amendments press constitutional theory to its limits in revolution. As the authors of the Declaration of Independence agreed, the right to revolution should not be exercised lightly. This consideration points in two directions

---

17 The theory of the constituent power raises questions about whether such procedures *must* be followed. Those questions parallel the ones addressed in the text.

for the theory of unconstitutional amendments. The doctrine erects legal barriers to the adoption of fundamental changes in a constitution's basic structures and so, might be thought to ensure that the constituent power exercises itself in that way only in the most pressing circumstances. Similarly, mechanisms for constitutional replacement, where they exist, typically are more cumbersome than those for constitutional amendment. The increased burden of replacing the existing constitution with another one might, again, limit replacements to truly important occasions.

The doctrine of substantive unconstitutionality of formally proper constitutional amendments raises in particularly acute form the general difficulty associated with constitutional review. Consider that candidates for inclusion in a constitution's basic structure are federalism, equality and secularism. The original constitution gives some meaning to those general concepts. A constitutional amendment dealing with federalism or secularism gives another meaning to them. The doctrine of unconstitutional amendments then leads to the question: Why should a constitutional court's specification of one general concept – even when imputed to the original constitution – prevail over another, reasonable alternative specification?[18] Various answers are possible in cases of ordinary constitutional review of statutes. For example, the legislative process might be flawed so that the nation's people as a whole are not fairly represented; or the court can claim to be acting in the service of the people constituted at the time the constitution was adopted, against the people who happen to occupy legislative positions when the statute at issue was enacted. These answers are much less readily available, if they are available at all, in connection with constitutional amendments adopted through constitutionally authorized procedures.

We can approach an answer by shifting attention from amendments that are said to be unconstitutional because they violate – or transform – general features of the basic structure, to amendments that are seemingly more focused. The Constitutional Court of Colombia's decisions on amendments dealing with the president's eligibility for re-election are quite instructive. Alvaro Uribe was a successful and quite popular president. Limited by the existing constitution to a single term in office, as is common in Latin America, Uribe sought and obtained a constitutional amendment allowing him to run for re-election. The

---

18 For additional discussion, see Chapter 3.

Constitutional Court held that this amendment was constitutionally permissible. Then, during his second term, Uribe sought an amendment allowing him to run for office a third time. The Constitutional Court held that this amendment would be unconstitutional.[19] The reason was that Colombian history and its institutional arrangements meant that the nation's commitment to electoral democracy might be threatened by a three-term president's accumulation of power.

The Colombian example suggests that the doctrine of substantive unconstitutionality might be quite context- and nation-specific. What might be a reasonable choice for some nations might be threatening to constitutionalism in others. So, for example, a specification of secularism's meaning that allowed some degree of state-religion interaction in one nation might be problematic in another nation. Constitutional courts might be sensitive to these contextual variables in a way that no doctrine could capture by anything other than the words "basic structure".

This suggestion might gain some support from the fact that decisions holding amendments substantively unconstitutional have often been accepted by the nation's people, who endorsed the amendments through appropriate procedures and the nation's political elites, some of whom sponsored those amendments. President Uribe, for example, vacated the office of the presidency when his second term expired. This behavior suggests that constitutional courts might be drawing up what political scientists call "diffuse support" for the courts. Diffuse support involves agreement with the proposition that the constitutional court properly exercises the power of constitutional review even in cases where people offering that support disagree with the court's decisions. Some modest support for the idea that diffuse support plays a role in stabilizing the doctrine of substantively unconstitutional amendments can be found in the fact that many amendments that have been found substantively unconstitutional have involved restrictions on the courts' ability to exercise the power of constitutional review.

The doctrine of substantive unconstitutionality might frustrate proponents of fundamental change who, in response, might resort to the right of revolution, with violence often attending. They might think

---

19 It is a matter of controversy among scholars of Colombian constitutional law whether the Court's decision rested on the proposition that the third-term amendment would be substantively unconstitutional.

that their amendment did not so much violate the existing constitution as transform it. Alternatively, the proponents might treat the obstacles to accomplishing their goal as pointless impediments, permissibly ignored. This might be particularly so where the thwarted amendment seems relatively discrete. In the term-limits case, for example, proponents might think that everything else about the constitution was quite acceptable, and be puzzled at being required to go through an elaborate process of constitutional replacement at the end of which is a "new" constitution identical, save for the term-limits provision, to the old one. Perhaps constitutional theory should treat an unconstitutional amendment as a pro tanto exercise of the right to revolution through the form of law, a form that allows fundamental change to occur without violence.

2.4.3   Deferring issues for future resolution

Recent work by Rosalind Dixon and Tom Ginsburg, as well as by Tsvi Kahana, has highlighted some structural features of substantive constitutional provisions (Ginsburg and Dixon 2011b; Kahana 2013). Constitution-writers resolve some core substantive issues but defer other, sometimes equally important, ones to the future. These deferrals come in various forms.

Perhaps the most familiar is the deferral of issues to constitutional courts. The authors of the Constitution of South Africa were personally committed to the abolition of capital punishment but were not in a position politically to include abolition in the constitution. They created a constitutional court and understood that that court would address capital punishment's constitutionality, as it did in the first case it decided.[20] Equality clauses often enumerate specific protected classes accompanied by a catch-all provision. The latter licenses later decision-makers, primarily courts, to decide whether some non-enumerated class should receive protection equivalent to that given the enumerated ones. Historically, the most important uses of catch-all provisions have involved gender. There the catch-all has been used because the constitution is old and difficult to amend, as in the United States. Sometimes, however, it occurs because the constitution-makers preferred deferring the issue to later resolution by another institution to resolving it themselves. This appears to be the case with some modern constitutions in connection with sexual orientation.

---

20 *State v. Makwanyane* [1995] ZACC 3, 1995 (3) SA 391 (CC), 1995 (6) BCLR 665 (CC).

Sometimes deferrals to the future occur for largely technical reasons. Consider the laws regulating election processes. Constitution-makers might be able to specify some basic choices, for example the choice between first-past-the-post plurality rules in individual districts or proportional representation of various sorts. Implementing those choices requires greater detail than is often achievable in the constitution-making process. Yet, the precise contours of electoral laws – and other statutes of similar importance – are typically almost as consequential as the choices embedded in the constitution. In part, constitution-makers can address these questions by specifying that some topics, such as the electoral rules, will be set by "organic laws" to be adopted by the legislature. Typically, the category of organic laws is defined by rules requiring their adoption – and, importantly, amendment or repeal – by a qualified majority of the legislature, sometimes a super-majority such as two-thirds, sometimes a majority of the body as a whole rather than a majority of a quorum.

Organic laws fall between ordinary legislation and constitutional provisions on a scale of difficulty of adoption, amendment and repeal. In addition to their utility in dealing with important subjects whose implementation is rife with technical detail, creating the category can be a useful mechanism for getting over some obstacles in the constitution-writing process, and the phenomenon of organic laws is common enough that constitution-writers may reasonably believe that they are not avoiding their responsibilities. Still, there are some hidden traps. Less important is the possibility that the constitution-writers will place too many laws in that category, perhaps out of a desire to get their work completed. Once adopted, the organic laws may be more resistant to alteration than appropriate for the subject matter.[21] More important, deferring issues to the legislature may simply put off political confrontations that might have been addressed at the constitution-writing stage but that might be destabilizing in the legislature.

Dixon and Ginsburg's study (2011b) focuses on another form of deferral – provisions that specify that some issues will be resolved "by law" rather than, implicitly, by the constitution itself. Here it is useful to distinguish between federal systems and non-federal (unitary) ones. Constitutions for federal systems must allocate power between the nation and subnational units. Exercises of the power allocated to the

---

21   As a hypothetical, consider a constitutional provision that an organic law will define the nation's bankruptcy laws.

national government will necessarily occur "by law" in some sense. Put another way, a "by law" clause accompanies every allocation of power to the national government. The US Constitution gives Congress the power "To establish ... uniform Laws on the subject of Bankruptcies ... ". The reference to "Laws" might seem to make this a "by law" clause, but in reality the bankruptcy clause is indistinguishable in this regard from the commerce clause that immediately precedes it, which makes no reference to "laws" regulating commerce among the several states.

"By law" clauses can have a function, other than deferral of decisions to the future, not addressed in detail by Dixon and Ginsburg. Consider a unitary system in which the national government has all the powers inherent in sovereignty. Saying that the national government shall act "by law" with respect to some subject adds nothing to the power of the government to be created by the constitution, and so does not defer any decision at all. A "by law" clause might serve to allocate power between the legislature, which enacts laws and the executive, which acts by decree, by secondary legislation (the term used in the United Kingdom), or by administrative "rule" (the term used in the United States). I note one difficulty with the use of "by law" clauses to allocate power between the legislature and the executive. Except with respect to prerogative powers – those inherent in the executive function itself – all executive action is ultimately authorized "by law". The British terminology is especially useful here, because it shows that legislatures enact primary legislation that executives then implement through secondary legislation.[22] A "by law" clause might not distinguish effectively between executive action taken pursuant to permissibly delegated authority and action that must be taken pursuant to quite specific laws. Indeed, again putting prerogative power to one side, no statute can be sufficiently detailed to resolve all questions "by law", implying that a "by law" clause will be subject to some pressure at the edges and perhaps even close to the core. The allocational function of "by law" clauses deserves more scholarly study.

Dixon examines another facet of the alternatives of drafting specificity and generality (Dixon, manuscript forthcoming). Sometimes constitutional specificity arises from one important function of new constitutions, that of repudiating abuses of the past. The South African

---

22 The US account of executive power, other than that inherent in the executive, as consisting of delegations from the legislature is to the same effect.

Constitution's detailed provisions laying out the procedures for pre-trial detention are an example. Specificity tightly confines future inter-preters, while generality licenses them to engage in more wide-ranging interpretation. Relying on evidence from cognitive science, Dixon argues that future interpreters – specifically, judges – might treat gen-erality as a signal that the constitution-writers trusted them to inter-pret the new constitution correctly and, as a result, will be inclined to do so in a reciprocal manner, that is, by interpreting it to reflect what the judges understand to be purposes the constitution-writers did not, or could not, effectively express in the document itself. The other side of the argument is that specific provisions may be taken to signal mis-trust of the future interpreters. A provision that stated that pretrial detention must be limited to a "reasonable" time before a court appear-ance might be interpreted to require an appearance within forty-eight hours of arrest, but a court attuned to interests in domestic security might adopt a more flexible standard. Fearing a return to the past they are seeking to repudiate, the constitution-writers attempt to tie interpreters' hands through linguistic specificity. Dixon suggests that this strategy may backfire: Interpreters who take generality as a signal of trust will then reciprocate, but interpreters who interpret specificity as a signal of mistrust may also reciprocate, this time by being quite grudging in their constitutional interpretations.

Dixon's argument is intriguing, but rests on what might turn out to be shaky foundations in its application of the findings of cognitive science, particularly in light of the extended time frame in which the supposed reciprocity effects are to occur. Consider first the years shortly after a constitution's adoption. There is likely to be a substantial overlap between the constitution-writers and its early interpreters. Memory might do much of the work that Dixon attributes to reciprocity. Reciprocity and its obverse might have some effects because the inter-preters engage in ongoing interactions with the constitution-writers. Suppose for example that the constitution-writers are suspicious about the capacity of judges chosen by the prior regime to interpret the con-stitution fairly. They might well insert as many specific provisions into the constitution as they can. Knowing of the constitution-writers' sus-picions, the interpreters may confirm them through grudging inter-pretation. Yet, here it may be unclear whether we are observing the psychological effects Dixon describes or the confirmation of the pre-dictive judgment the constitution-writers made. Now consider con-stitutional interpretation over the longer term. The interpreters may invoke what we can call the "What's he to Hecuba?" principle. That is, the constitution-writers have passed from the scene, it is unclear why interpreters should now be concerned with reciprocating the trust or mistrust exhibited by the constitution-writers.

Dixon suggests that principles of reciprocity can help us understand what she calls optimal constitutional design, that is, design that combines specificity and generality to produce optimal levels of flexibility and rigidity when the constitution's provisions are implemented.[23] That certainly is a desirable feature for constitutions to have, but whether cognitive science provides better guidance than Hamilton's "reflection and choice" seems open to question.

Tsvi Kahana (2013) has begun work on a project related to Dixon's. Discussing the process by which the Basic Law: Freedom of Occupation was amended in 1994 and evoking John Marshall's opinion in *McCulloch v. Maryland*,[24] Kahana distinguishes between a "majestic" constitution and a more mundane one. A majestic constitution contains truly fundamental provisions of a sort that can inspire loyalty among the nation's citizens; a mundane one is filled with technical detail and has, as Richard Hofstadter (1973) said of Abraham Lincoln's Emancipation Proclamation, "all the moral grandeur of a bill of lading". As the reference to *McCulloch* suggests, the distinction between the majestic and the mundane does not map directly on to a distinction between rights-granting and power-conferring constitutional provisions. And, as the earlier mention of the South African provision on pre-arraignment detention suggests, neither does it map directly on to a distinction between the general and the specific; for the South African provision, understood against its historical background, is a majestic one. More work needs to be done here as well, but Kahana's insight about the majestic and the mundane is likely to prove generative.

2.5 Why comply with the constitution?

It would seem obvious that people who adopt a constitution ought to comply with it. And, perhaps that is true of the very generation that

---

23 As with many issues of constitutional design, this one is bound up with questions about the amendment formula: Specificity that turns out to be undesirable may be altered pursuant to amendment, but the ease with which that can occur depends on the amendment rule (and similarly with generality).

24 17 US (4 Wheaton) 316 (1819).

does adopt a constitution. Yet, the question of compliance arises both normatively and descriptively. The problem occurs when someone – especially a majority short of the supermajority required to amend the constitution – finds that some constitutional arrangement in place blocks them from achieving a policy goal they think desirable. Suppose they agree that stability in constitutional arrangements is an important value, but, after taking that into account, they think that, on balance, their nation would be better overall if it violated the constitution and adopted the policy. Are there good reasons for abandoning the policy anyway (Seidman 2012)?

There is a standard catalogue of reasons for complying with a constitution once it has been adopted. The constitution sets up a regular scheme for making policy decisions and adhering to it, conserves political energy: Instead of having to decide first (and recurrently) what structure for making a policy decision to use, people can immediately decide the policy questions that animate them. An entrenched constitutional structure enables longer term planning than would a "merely" conventional agreement to put some differences aside for the moment. Knowing how the constitution works, people can coordinate their actions in light of what they expect will happen within that structure. Constitutions might include compromises that allow people to set aside some of their divisions to work on problems where, they hope, they can come to some relatively permanent agreement. (And, perhaps, the experience of working together on such problems will lead them to believe that the divisions that seemed important earlier are not truly important.)

All of these are reasons for having a constitution and complying with it *generally*. Yet, the question of compliance arises only when some group finds itself disadvantaged on a matter of deep concern when, the group's members believe, adhering to the constitution is blocking them from achieving their policy goal. Under these circumstances, why might they comply with the constitution nevertheless? Why should they?

One consideration might be that reopening a decision made as part of a larger package could lead others to try to reopen other decisions, ultimately producing severe instability, especially if the reopened provision resulted from compromises that remain important in preserving the constitution's stability. Note, though, that if this is true, the proper all-things-considered judgment would be to abandon the policy goal that generated the noncompliance with the constitution. Still, people might be imperfect calculators, underestimating the risk that others will start questioning other constitutional settlements. A related point is that the constitution might be working "acceptably" overall, even if it occasionally blocks the adoption of valuable policies. The political effort needed to gain agreement that the policy difficulty flows from one or a few identifiable constitutional provisions, coupled with the political effort needed to adopt the policy, may lead people to treat the obstacle as one of the occasional costs of operating the constitution for the government's daily operations. Of course, this analysis would lose a great deal of force were the policy being blocked regarded by its proponents as a truly important one.

Ignoring the constitution might prove impossible in practice. Some provisions, such as those dealing with some electoral arrangements, can lead political actors to pursue specific paths and give them an interest in preserving the constitution to which they have adapted institutionally as well as psychologically (Levinson 2011).

2.6   Conclusion

This chapter is replete with generalizations and qualifications. The qualifications are as important as the generalizations. The issues identified here do not create difficulties in every constitution-making process and some processes – probably unusually – may go quite smoothly. The issues' structural dynamics are built in, but the dynamics may not always affect constitution-making because specific circumstances keep them suppressed. The idea of the constituent power plays an important part in thinking about some but not all of the issues, but that idea sometimes serves a purely conceptual end, clarifying some important questions and yet, sometimes seems to be tied to ideas about the actual participation and consent of a nation's people in constitution-making.

Constitution-makers face a range of pressures from the specific historical conditions under which they act. Perhaps they can improve their performance merely by being aware of typical issues: What might seem to them unique problems might actually be common ones and thinking about how other constitution-makers have dealt with those problems, may help them in their own endeavors. As Oliver Wendell Holmes observed: "When you get the dragon out of his cave on to the plain and in the daylight, you can count his teeth and claws, and see just what is his strength" (Holmes, 1897: 469). This chapter has tried to identify some of the dragons that inhabit the cave of constitution-making.

3 The structures of constitutional review and some implications for substantive constitutional law

3.1 Introduction

Among the important issues of constitutional design today is that of the structures of constitutional review.[1] Historically a central question about constitutional design was whether to have a system of parliamentary supremacy or a system in which primary legislation was subject to review in some court for consistency with the constitution. Parliamentary supremacy did not exclude the courts entirely from enforcing the constitution. They could hold executive action unlawful where the action violated what the courts found to be fundamental rights *and* was unauthorized by legislation (the latter condition is known in common law constitutional theory as the *ultra vires* ("beyond power") doctrine). And, they could hold delegated legislation – known by various names, such as "administrative rules" in the United States, "secondary legislation" in the United Kingdom and "decree-laws" in other systems – unlawful on the same two grounds: that it violated fundamental rights and was unauthorized by primary legislation. Further, courts could insist on a rather high degree of specificity in the authorization for executive action or secondary legislation depending on how serious they believed the infringement on fundamental rights. The key characteristic of systems of parliamentary supremacy, however, was that courts could not find unlawful primary legislation, executive action expressly authorized by primary legislation, or secondary legislation similarly authorized.

---

1 The terminology to describe the practice of authorizing courts to determine whether legislation is constitutional varies. In the United States the practice is known as judicial review, which in other common law systems is a term used for review of administrative action. In many civil law countries the practice is known as judicial control of constitutionality. I use the term *constitutional review* to refer to the practice.

Systems of constitutional review add to all these possibilities the further one that courts can find primary legislation unlawful. Essentially all modern constitutions reject parliamentary supremacy in favor of some form of constitutional review, with New Zealand the only system that remains committed in theory to parliamentary supremacy. (The United Kingdom and Israel are candidates for systems still committed to parliamentary supremacy, but the best analysis of those nations' systems is that they now have some form of constitutional review.) The contemporary issues of constitutional design, then, deal with the form of constitutional review, not whether to have it.

3.2   Establishing constitutional review

That constitutional review has triumphed is uncontroversial; *why* it has triumphed requires some explanation. The best scholarly accounts focus on a variety of so-called "insurance" models of constitutional review (Hirschl 2004; Stephenson 2003). The core idea in these models is that political parties seek to sustain their power even after they have lost control over legislative and executive offices. Consider a political party whose leaders expect to be displaced by the opposition within a relatively short period. They can entrench their policies by creating a court with the power to invalidate new policies inconsistent with those the now-ousted party has enacted. The court serves as insurance for the party's policies against the day when the party itself has lost office – at least if the expected tenure of the court's judges is long enough.

The insurance model just sketched deals with a transitional period, when one party sees itself about to lose office after a long period of dominance (the period being long enough for it to entrench its policies in the constitution). It has some direct empirical support (Hirschl 2004) and some indirect empirical support in the observation that constitutional courts in nations (still) dominated by a single party are rarely "activist".

Constitutional review is expressly authorized in contemporary constitutions, whether through the creation of a constitutional court or by conferring the power of constitutional review on a generalist court. That constitutional review is authorized, however, does not mean that it will be effectively exercised. As noted above, courts in nations where a single political party dominates the system for an extended period rarely find national legislation unconstitutional.

Establishing constitutional review as an *effective* practice in other types of political systems, even where the formal practice is expressly authorized, is not always a forgone conclusion. The reason, of course, is that effective constitutional review entails placing the court exercising the power in conflict with those holding political power in the nation at the moment the court decides. Courts have some resources – for example, general support among the public and the fact that, where there are competing political parties, a ruling against the presently governing party may find support among the opposition. Still, exercising the power of constitutional review places the court at some risk. The government party can retaliate by limiting the court's jurisdiction, restricting its budget thereby worsening the judges' working conditions, mounting a public campaign against the judges and so on.

We can identify two "strategies" judges on constitutional courts might use to embed the institution of constitutional review into the overall system of governance. The first strategy might be called "one and done". Here the court takes up one extremely important and politically controversial question early in its existence, and resolves it against the then-ruling party or coalition. Doing so will generate a fair amount of resentment and criticism of the court, precisely because the issue is an important one. To avoid compounding the court's political vulnerability, the court recedes. After the first controversial decision it does no more for a while. It might of course uphold national statutes as constitutionally permissible, but it does not confront the government again on an important matter. From a strategic point of view, this allows the controversy over the initial decision to recede into the background. If the court survives the first confrontation, a decade later it might be in a position to say that its power of constitutional review has already been established and accepted by the political system as a whole. The court can then make exercises of its power routine.

The "one and done" strategy requires that some issues of constitutional interpretation on a matter important to the national governing party or coalition come before the court relatively early in its existence. It is probably best illustrated by the US Supreme Court's decision in *Marbury v. Madison*.[2] The conventional account is that the Court, having shown that it could find national statutes unconstitutional in a politically controversial case, then refrained from doing so for nearly a

---

2 5 US (1 Cranch) 137 (1803).

half century.[3] When it returned to the task, it could and did treat the power of constitutional review as firmly established.

A slightly different example is provided by South Africa. There the Constitutional Court issued an early decision holding that President Nelson Mandela had acted unconstitutionally when he remitted the sentences of mothers with primary responsibility for the care of young children but not the sentences of fathers with such responsibility.[4] President Mandela promptly issued a statement saying that he would comply with the decision because he believed that doing so would place South Africa's practice of constitutional review on a firm footing.

The standard example of the risks posed by repeated early confrontations on important matters is the Russian Constitutional Court in the early 1990s, whose decisions on extremely contentious matters involving presidential power and federalism led to the court's suspension for several years (Sharlet 1993).

The alternative strategy is incremental and relatively continuous. From the beginning the court regularly invalidates relatively minor national statutes. These decisions are unlikely to attract much attention from the political branches. Politicians get accustomed to the practice of constitutional review. A later intervention on a matter the politicians believe important can then be defended as simply the exercise of a power whose routine use has already been accepted by the political system as a whole.

Calling these ways of establishing the effective power of constitutional review "strategies" suggests that the choices are conscious and sometimes they may be, at least in part. More likely, though, the strategies seem to the judges the natural way of doing things. Notably, the "one and done" strategy requires that a politically contentious and important constitutional issue come before the constitutional court early in its existence. Under modern conditions that might be nearly

---

3 The standard account has been questioned by scholars who have pointed to numerous decisions between 1803 and 1857 in the which the US Supreme Court construed statutes to be constitutional after determining that, were the statutes to be construed otherwise, they would be unconstitutional, thereby interpreting the Constitution as applied to national statutes (Graber 2007; Whittington 2009). These opinions did not, though, pose the same risk of political retaliation as would opinions holding the statutes unconstitutional.

4 *President of the Republic of South Africa v. Hugo* [1997] ZACC 4.

inevitable, but the opportunities provided for the incremental strategy are truly inevitable.

For nations where political parties regularly rotate in office, the account is less of the establishment than of the maintenance of constitutional review. In such systems every party can expect to benefit, sometimes, from constitutional review and the constitutional court is itself, likely to have support from *some* party no matter what it does. As a result, constitutional courts in these systems have a large amount of leeway in interpreting the constitution.

3.3   Political constitutionalism as an alternative to constitutional review in the courts

Although eliminating constitutional review conducted in some form by courts is probably not a realistic possibility anywhere and designers of new constitutions almost always include some form of such review in their designs,[5] it is worth considering what might be said in favor of an older tradition of parliamentary supremacy within a constitutional system. Parliamentary supremacy means that parliament itself makes the ultimate determination about whether one of its own enactments violates the constitution. One common reaction to that definition treats it as almost self-refuting: It is, the argument goes, like putting the fox to guard the chicken-coop. Parliament enacts the statute at issue, so why would it ever find its own enactment unconstitutional?

The adoption of written constitutions understood to enact law supreme over ordinary legislation placed pressure on the theory of parliamentary supremacy. Toward the end of the twentieth century some constitutional theorists developed a reasonably robust theory reconciling parliamentary supremacy with the supremacy of the constitution. They described a "political constitutionalism" (the term used mostly in connection with the United Kingdom) or a "popular constitutionalism" (the term used in the United States) (Bellamy 2007; Ewing, Campbell and Tomkins 2001; Tushnet 1999; Kramer 2005).

Political constitutionalism began as a theory offered by leftist critics of constitutional review conducted by the courts. Some, especially in

---

5 The possibility that the British Parliament will repeal the Human Rights Act 1998 and revert to a system of pure parliamentary supremacy is small, though not zero.

the United Kingdom, were concerned that authorizing the courts to invalidate legislation would generate anti-redistributive results (as it had in the United States in the early twentieth century) because of the assumed conservatism of judges. Others were concerned that constitutional review in the courts would hold out a false hope to leftists that they could achieve in the courts what they could not achieve through political action and so, might divert their efforts from political organizing to litigation (Mandel 1989). The motivation in the United States was more obviously political: The US Supreme Court, which had been an ally of liberals in the 1960s and 1970s, became a reasonably reliable ally of conservatives thereafter. "Taking the Constitution Away from the Courts" (Tushnet 1999) would deprive conservatives of a weapon they were wielding with great success in what were essentially political controversies. But, whatever its origins in politics, political constitutionalism is an account of institutional design in a constitutional state that warrants evaluation on its merits.

One way of understanding the theory of political constitutionalism is to think through its response to the fox-and-chicken-coop question. For political constitutionalists, that question arises only because the person asking it focuses on the wrong moment in time – after a statute is enacted. Political constitutionalists argue that analysis should focus on the period before enactment, when the legislature is considering whether to enact a statute. They begin with some important qualifying suppositions. Suppose the legislature's attention is directed to constitutional questions about a proposed statute, and suppose as well that the legislature deliberates responsibly about the merits of those questions. Political constitutionalists argue that under those conditions it is well-nigh impossible that legislation would be enacted that beyond question violates constitutional restraints on government.

Skeptics (or cynics) about the legislative process often express doubt that legislators *will* deliberate seriously about the constitution or, as I will also put it, be constitutionally conscientious. Perhaps Burkean representatives, who take their job to be enacting policies in the nation's long-term interests, would be constitutionally conscientious, because, such representatives might think, the constitution itself is in the nation's long-term interest. But what of representatives who think of themselves as the "mere" voices for their constituents' desires or interests, or, worse, who consider only how their votes on proposals will affect their re-election prospects? The positions such legislators take derive from their constituents' views, not from their own thinking about the constitution and so, the argument goes, they will not be constitutionally conscientious.

Political constitutionalists have several responses: (1) The cynical view of legislators rests on the wrong set of policies legislatures consider. Legislators may vote on proposals about building roads and other infrastructure based on their judgment about how those proposals will affect their constituents and therefore their prospects for re-election: Vote for a proposal that provides material benefits to the constituents, against one that does not. Or they will vote based on how proposals affect important interest groups or campaign contributors whose material interests will benefit from (or be hurt by) the proposals. Political constitutionalists concede the truth of these observations, but note that the legislative proposals at issue rarely raise important issues of constitutional law. For them, the observations, even if true, are largely irrelevant.

(2) More important, if the constituents' views are themselves based on the constitution, the legislators' derivative views will be as well and that makes the legislators constitutionally conscientious. And on many important issues this may well be true. To use examples from the United States: Voters' views about abortion, gay rights, gun rights, campaign finance and affirmative action – central issues in contemporary constitutional debates there – are based on their reasoning about competing constitutional values and not, for example, about personal self-interest in the ordinary sense. Of course many voters come to conclusions about the constitution's meaning that are different from the conclusions reached by constitutional courts, or by scholars of constitutional law, but that does not mean that the voters' views are "wrong", only that they are different. For political constitutionalists, the meaning of constitutional terms often lies within a range of reasonable disagreement and the differences between voters' views and scholars' reflect nothing more than that fact.

Party competition is an important mechanism for ensuring that legislators' views will in fact derive from those of their constituents, with respect to the constitution as much as with respect to legislation that provides voters (or interest groups or campaign contributors) material benefits. A legislator who fails to represent constituents' views may face an opponent in the next election who makes the legislator's constitutional views a campaign issue.

(3) Sometimes constituents will have no constitutional views on legislative proposals. Political constitutionalists argue that we can understand this situation in two ways, both of which let the legislator be constitutionally conscientious. Constituents can be seen as delegating responsibility for thinking about the constitution's meaning to the representative (and may discipline the legislator at the next election if the legislator acts irresponsibly). Or, they can be seen as indifferent to the constitution, leaving the legislator free to be Burkean.

The possibility that a conscientious legislature will overlook constitutional questions lurking in proposed statutes poses a real difficulty for political constitutionalism. For example, a problematic provision might be embedded deep within a much larger statute, whose policy dimensions garner the legislature's entire attention. We can design institutions to reduce this difficulty, in the form of a "legislation-vetting" agency that evaluates the constitutionality of proposed legislation. The United Kingdom, Japan and Sweden have versions of these agencies. The United Kingdom's mechanism has some parts in the executive ministries and others in parliament, while Japan's is located within the legislature. Sweden's is located outside the government: Sometimes the government will consult academic experts about constitutional questions and defer to their judgments.

The reasons for creating these institutions vary. Conscientious legislatures, knowing the risk that they will overlook constitutional questions, could create the institutions because of their very conscientiousness. One important reason lies outside the domain of political constitutionalism. The institutions may be created and used to reduce the possibility that the government will be embarrassed when the courts invalidate an important piece of legislation. But if legislators are not conscientious enough, they might have no incentives to create legislation-vetting institutions.

Political constitutionalism is in theory a viable alternative to constitutional review in the courts, but it is not a practicably achievable mechanism under modern conditions. The arguments against strong skepticism about the possibility of responsible legislative deliberation about the constitution have some weight, but on the whole those arguments describe possibilities and so do not completely overcome the skeptical or cynical case. By offering some counterweight to strong arguments for *judicial* constitutionalism, the arguments that underpin political constitutionalism may have some bearing on designing mechanisms for constitutional review in the courts and on the approach constitutional courts should take to the task of evaluating the consistency of legislative enactments with the constitution. Political constitutionalism may be better as a justification for generous standards of constitutional review – reasonableness rather than proportionality, for example – than as a free-standing account of modern constitutionalism.

3.4   The classical issues in the structure of constitutional review

For much of the history of constitutional review the structural issues involved a choice between two general models – one provided by the United States, the other developed by the Austrian jurist Hans Kelsen after the First World War.

The US model was the first and for over a century essentially the only model available. It has several features, not all of which are logically linked. First, constitutional review is dispersed through the judicial system. Every court – or nearly every one – has the power to find primary legislation unconstitutional. Second, and as an immediate consequence, constitutional review is not confined to a *specialized* constitutional court – that is, a court whose sole jurisdiction is to deal with constitutional questions. Rather, constitutional review is exercised by courts that also engage in other judicial activities, notably interpreting statutes and developing private law.[6] Third, constitutional review can be triggered by a wide range of litigants rather than a restricted list. The United States requires that a person seeking to trigger constitutional review have "standing", which the US Supreme Court has interpreted to mean that the person be injured by the action he or she claims to be unconstitutional, and that the injury already have occurred or is quite likely to occur. Other nations that use the US model have quite broad rules of standing, to the point where it is better to describe them as systems in which almost anyone is entitled to trigger constitutional review, with quite narrow exceptions.

---

6 The US system of federalism introduces complexities with respect to the development of private law, because under the prevailing account of constitutional power in the United States, private law is generally to be developed by courts appointed by the subnational authorities – the "states" – and not by the national courts. Those complexities are not inherent in the US model of constitutional review and they are ignored in this chapter.

These features have implications for conceptualizing constitutional review and for judicial selection. As to conceptualizing constitutional review: In systems adopting the US model or slight variants, constitutional review is understood to be continuous with ordinary legal practices of statutory interpretation and the development of private law. In this model constitutional review, which involves the interpretation of the constitution, is a species of the more general practice of ordinary legal interpretation. There are two implications for judicial selection. Those who exercise constitutional review must have the capacity to engage in ordinary legal interpretation. As a shorthand, we can say that they should be judges first, primarily in terms of the way that they think about their duties when interpreting the constitution, but secondarily – with respect to judges in the highest courts – in terms of the training they receive before taking that position. In addition, they should not think of constitutional review as some sort of extraordinary practice, but as simply legal. Importantly, they should not think that constitutional review implicates some distinctively *political* mode of thinking. They might acknowledge that interpreting statutes and developing the private law might have some "political" or policy component, as American legal realists and critical legal theorists emphasized, but nevertheless the judges should not think that constitutional interpretation has some *different* political or policy component.

Kelsen developed the second model because he believed that constitutional review did have a distinctively political component. His thinking was shaped by the understanding, sensible at the time but now outdated, that the primary role of constitutions was to establish a framework of government, with the protection of fundamental rights having at most a small role. With that understanding, Kelsen believed that constitutional conflicts would arise over the allocation of authority among the institutions the constitution created – between the president and the parliament, for example. Those conflicts, he further believed, would inevitably have an important political component. They would arise out of mundane political conflicts, but their resolution would require choices about deeper political-theoretical matters involving estimates of the relative power of the institutions in conflict, over the long run and with respect to different issues.

Kelsen's design for a constitutional court built the political elements of the resolution of this sort of constitutional conflict into its structure. First, the power of constitutional review should be concentrated in a single court. Perhaps Kelsen may have thought that the institution whose role was to resolve conflicts between major institutions should also have the kind of stature they had, though the institutional logic for that conclusion is weak. Any institution, including a system of dispersed judicial review, would gain an ally (and make an enemy) when it resolved a conflict: A ruling against the president would please the parliament, one against the parliament would please the president.

Probably more important in justifying a centralized system of constitutional review was a second element. The political contours of the issues the constitutional court would face meant that members of the constitutional court should have some degree of political experience and sensitivity.[7] They should not be *merely* judges. But, coming from a civil law tradition, Kelsen saw ordinary judges as likely to lack the requisite political sensitivity. Such judges would not do well at the task of constitutional review, with its political elements. So, constitutional review could not be dispersed through the ordinary judicial system as in the US model.

Other components of the Kelsenian model also flowed from its assumptions about the nature of the issues the constitutional court would deal with. The issues were such that access to the constitutional court should be limited – to the president, parliamentary officials and the like. The feature here is of limited rather than broad access, not the exact list of those authorized to invoke constitutional review. And, finally, the issues were such that the constitutional questions could be identified rather easily: Did a president have the power to issue a decree of this sort, or did the legal rule embodied in the decree have to be expressed in a statute enacted by parliament? Did a subnational government have the power to enact a law on this topic, or was the subject one over which the national government had exclusive jurisdiction? In the Kelsenian model these issues could be resolved by inspecting the statutes and the constitution without knowing much if anything about how the statutes or decrees would actually operate in practice. Constitutional review could be *a priori*, that is, could occur before the statutes or decrees took effect, and the constitutional court would exercise only what Kelsen described as a "negative" power – a power to block the adoption of a statute or decree but no power, even in an indirect or advisory way, to influence

---

7 The clearest example of the place political sensitivity holds in the Kelsenian vision is the rule that former presidents of France are entitled to sit on the Constitutional Council even if they have no legal training.

the shape of statutes or decrees to bring them into conformity with the constitution.

The Kelsenian model was widely adopted after the Second World War, mostly in systems strongly influenced by the civil law tradition, but the US model remained available and was adopted elsewhere, mostly in systems with a strong common law heritage. Changes in the issues that constitutional courts faced and changes in understanding about how constitutional review could contribute to a well-functioning government, began to reshape courts that initially were designed on the US and on the Kelsenian models.

Probably the most important change arose from a shift in the focus of constitutional review. For much of US history and expressly in the Kelsenian model, constitutional review involved primarily issues of government structure. At some point in the twentieth century the focus of constitutional review changed to concern about violations of fundamental individual rights.[8] The new focus had important implications for the Kelsenian model. Most important, mechanisms had to be developed that would allow claims about violations of individual rights to be brought to the constitutional court. Limited access to constitutional courts on the Kelsenian model meant that sometimes an obviously substantial claim that a new statute violated some fundamental right might never be brought to the court – when, for example, large majorities in all the parties supported a statute that targeted an unpopular minority.[9] In Kelsen's constitutional universe constitutional courts dealt with conflicts among the nation's governing institutions and members of those institutions – that is, those on the list of entities who had access to the constitutional court – had an incentive arising from their interest in preserving "their" institution's power to bring conflicts before that court. (But recent scholarship has strongly

---

8   The change was gradual, with individual rights increasingly important in the United States in the years before the Second World War, important in established liberal democracies in the years after 1945, and important everywhere once democratization took hold after decolonization, the wave of democratization in Latin America in the 1970s and the collapse of the Soviet empire near the end of the twentieth century.

9   The best recent example is the 2004 French legislation limiting the wearing of headscarves or other "ostentatious" religious objects in schools. The statute was enacted by such a large majority that the required sixty legislators could not be found to challenge the statute. Interestingly, although legislation adopted in 2010 banning the wearing of full facial coverings in public was adopted by similarly large margins, its *supporters* agreed to bring the statute before the Constitutional Council.

questioned whether the idea of institutional self-interest has any (real purchase in a world of political parties and strong ties between chief executives and legislators from the same party (Levinson and Pildes 2006)). In contrast, no similar institutional self-interest gives those with authorized access an incentive to use that access to raise questions about a statute's consistency with fundamental rights. Sometimes the legislative minority might have a contingent political interest in doing so, but the rise of a human rights culture meant that stronger institutional mechanisms were needed to get rights-issues before the Kelsenian constitutional court.

In addition, sometimes statutes violate fundamental rights only when they are applied to particular fact-situations. The *a priori* feature of the Kelsenian constitutional court thwarts consideration of such problems and the defect cannot be remedied fully by a vigorous application of administrative review and the *ultra vires* doctrine.

Systems that had adopted the Kelsenian model adapted to these new conditions by creating mechanisms for review of individual cases – individual complaints to the constitutional court or decisions on questions referred to the constitutional court after they had arisen in ordinary litigation. Notably, both forms of review were consistent with the Kelsenian commitment to a centralized and specialized constitutional court: The ordinary courts had to *refer* cases to the constitutional court rather than decide the constitutional issues and have their decisions *reviewed* by that court.

These new mechanisms, however, created another conflict, known generically as the "battle of the courts" – the parties in conflict being the constitutional courts and the highest level of ordinary courts. The battle occurs when the ordinary courts believe that the constitutional court is intruding on a domain reserved to them, the interpretation of statutes and the development of ordinary law. And, indeed it often is. The constitutional court may find a statute constitutional but only if it is interpreted in a specified way, and that interpretation is not the one lawyers would choose were they to use only the tools of ordinary statutory interpretation. Or the constitutional court says that the ordinary courts have applied private law in a way that is not sufficiently sensitive to constitutional values, and sends the issue back to the ordinary courts for them to apply private law in a more constitution-sensitive way. Importantly, the ordinary courts are not wrong in observing that these kinds of decisions by the constitutional court are not "purely" constitutional.

The outcomes of the battles of the courts are complex. Typically, the constitutional courts win the battles on the level of formal constitutional theory. But their victories are limited, as they acknowledge – or concede – that their supervision of the ordinary courts will occur with a relatively light hand. Oversimplifying: The constitutional courts defer to the ordinary courts' reasonable applications of constitutional law even if the constitutional courts acting on their own would have reached a different conclusion – but the constitutional courts occasionally intervene to displace a concededly reasonable position taken by the ordinary courts, essentially to demonstrate that their theoretical victory can sometimes be translated into a practical one.

The reason the constitutional courts use a light hand in supervising the ordinary courts is clear. To do otherwise, that is, to intervene aggressively to insist that the ordinary courts always reach the result the constitutional court would have reached, would substantially expand the jurisdiction and, importantly, the workload of the constitutional court.

The reasons for the other component – the constitutional courts' victory on the level of theory – are less clear. Among them probably is the relative prestige of the courts and, were the constitutional courts to be seen as overly "political", perhaps that advantage would disappear.

Interestingly, the constitutional courts can lose the battle of the courts when the ordinary courts can draw upon some support from outside the national judicial system. The examples to date come from Europe, where sometimes the ordinary courts can point to decisions by transnational courts that support the substantive positions they have taken, against the positions taken by the constitutional courts. (Stone-Sweet and Stranz 2012).

Creating an individual complaint system has other structural implications. Most constitutional systems have some notion of "justiciability", a term that seeks to classify cases into those that are and those that are not suitable for judicial resolution. The US model and the Kelsenian model augmented by an individual complaint system strain the idea of justiciability. Historically the idea of justiciability derived from the idea that there was a prerogative power in the government to act in disregard of the law, usually in emergency situations but sometimes more expansively in connection with a so-called "dispensing" power to set otherwise applicable law aside. The idea of a prerogative power is in deep tension with the idea that the constitution is a higher law that regulates all government action, so the idea itself has become controversial.

The idea of justiciability, however, persists, attended by controversy. Political actors sometimes seek to insulate their actions from review by the courts – and thereby to enable the possibility that their actions are inconsistent with the constitution – through clauses that oust the courts of jurisdiction.[10]

Another method for insulating government actions from scrutiny by the courts is the doctrine of "standing", which identifies those individuals or entities that are entitled to trigger constitutional scrutiny in the courts. We could describe the classic Kelsenian model as limiting standing to designated entities such as the president or parliamentarians. With an individual complaint mechanism added to the Kelsenian model, and in the US model from the beginning, courts considered *who* could trigger constitutional review. Typically the answer refers to some idea of injury, in a restrictive sense: Only those "injured" by government action can challenge its constitutionality.

Recent decisions of the US Supreme Court have suggested that the doctrine of standing inevitably restricts constitutional review. Notably, however, some constitutional courts allow citizen actions, or "public interest" actions as they are known in India. Other systems authorize specific institutions – ombuds offices or public prosecutors – to bring any constitutional claim to court. Courts are also willing to recognize "third-party" standing, the entitlement of someone who is not injured in the ordinary sense to take the place of a person who is, usually on the ground that the person suffering the injury cannot as a practical matter bring a lawsuit, for example because of poverty. Even in the United States the practical effect of the standing doctrine is limited, largely because "injury" tends to be defined broadly. (The restrictive US cases can be roughly summarized as holding only that those whose sole complaint is that the government has failed to comply with the law lack standing.)

Justiciability doctrines also include a doctrine referred to in the United States as the political questions doctrine and in other systems as an aspect of the separation of powers, here the division of authority between the courts and the political branches. The idea is that some

---

10 In British constitutional theory these are referred to as privative clauses.

constitutional questions are inextricable from fundamental policy and political judgments, making it inappropriate for the courts to say anything about them. Kelsen's understanding of the subject matter of constitutional review was that all constitutional questions could be resolved only with reference to *some* policy and political elements, which implies that these doctrines can refer to only a subset of all constitutional questions. Again with some exceptions, the political questions doctrine operates in two domains, foreign affairs and national security, and areas involving substantial public expenditure. Some courts treat some constitutional questions arising in these domains as non-justiciable. Others say that the very idea that the constitution is the nation's highest law requires that courts have the power to evaluate the constitutionality of every government action. These courts treat actions in these domains as justiciable. But, typically, they will apply a standard of review – sometimes described as reasonableness review – that is quite deferential to the policy judgments of the political branches. The courts will resolve the constitutional questions, but in doing so they will be sensitive to foreign policy or budgetary implications. Note, however, that deference and sensitivity do not mean abdication of a judicial role: Deferential courts will sometimes find actions within the two domains unconstitutional.

The political-question component of justiciability returns us to one of Kelsen's themes, that the judges on the constitutional courts ought to have some degree of political experience because they will be handling questions that, though questions of law, have important policy and political elements to them. Kelsen's critics described his position as entailing the judicialization of politics, and suggested that regular exercise of the power of constitutional review in politically contentious cases would lead to the politicization of the judiciary. This might be tolerable in, and even built into, the Kelsenian model, because the politicization of the judiciary would be limited to the constitutional court itself. It is more troubling in US model systems, where it would affect judges at every level of the system. Perhaps that would be a reason for more robust justiciability doctrines in systems adopting the US model.

Finally, as suggested earlier, contemporary systems of constitutional review are not always fully self-contained. Transnational courts, such as the two European courts and the Inter-American Court of Human Rights, change the incentives within domestic constitutional courts subject to "review" by those courts. The tendency seems to be for the domestic court to try to anticipate what the transnational court will do, even when the transnational court's decisions are not automatically given domestic validity and even when, as is sometimes true, the domestic constitution asserts that it is superior to treaties (which are the basis for the jurisdiction of the transnational courts).

Again, the structural explanations for this pattern are unclear. Attempting to anticipate the transnational court may avoid some degree of international embarrassment through a "reversal" – as it may be portrayed – or criticism by the transnational court. Doing so also provides the domestic court with some defenses against charges of usurping power, by allowing it to explain that it has acted simply to preempt the inevitable criticism by the transnational court. Still, the effects could go in the other direction. Criticism by the transnational court might generate resentment at the interference with domestic sovereignty going beyond what was agreed to in the treaty creating the transnational court's jurisdiction. And the domestic court could also pass responsibility off to the transnational court, which would allow domestic political authorities a wider range of choice about whether or how to accept the transnational court's judgment than would exist were the domestic court to rely entirely on domestic sources of law.

3.5   New structures of constitutional review

Constitutional review necessarily involves the displacement of executive or legislative judgments; those judgments can often plausibly be described as reflecting the views of a nation's majority as expressed through voting; and constitutional court judges are typically, at most, indirectly responsible to the electorate. These propositions generate the so-called countermajoritarian difficulty, examined in introductions to constitutional theory. Theorists have developed a number of elaborations of and responses to the countermajoritarian difficulty in constitutional theory itself.

The countermajoritarian difficulty arises when judges exercise the power of constitutional review, and a brief comment on why they might do so seems appropriate. That question rarely receives sustained attention, perhaps because the possible answers are obvious, though they might have some non-obvious implications. One view might be called cynical (or realistic): Constitutional court judges are like all other public officials, receiving benefits – mostly psychological – from exercising the power they have, to the extent that they can do so. Another view might be called idealistic (or realistic as well): Constitutional court judges do what they can to promote good governance.

The late twentieth century saw an important development in structures of constitutional review that was responsive, sometimes by design and sometimes by accident, to the countermajoritarian difficulty. The development has various labels: dialogic review (Hogg and Bushell 1997), weak-form constitutional review (Tushnet 2008), the new Commonwealth model of judicial review (Gardbaum 2013).

Dialogic review generally takes the following schematic form:

(1)   The legislature enacts a statute;
(2)   The statute is challenged before the constitutional court;
(3)   The constitutional court holds the statute unconstitutional.

To this point the process is identical to classical constitutional review. In that classic form there is only one possible response in the short run – a step 4 of amending the constitution. Dialogic review offers another possibility at step 4. The legislature can respond to the court's actions at step 3 by re-enacting the statute by a majority short of the supermajority typically required to amend the constitution.

Probably the best elaborated and theorized example is the Canadian "override" mechanism or its Section 33 power, which gives Canadian legislatures the power to make their statutes effective notwithstanding selected rights provisions in the Canadian Charter of Rights and Freedoms. They can do so by ordinary majority vote, but the "override" statute sunsets within five years, a period made significant by the fact that Canadian law requires at least one election in every five-year period. A legislature's use of the override power can be made a subject of political contestation at the next election after its use. Some constitutional rights cannot be overridden; the most important for comparative purposes is the right to vote.

The override power fits comfortably with the general structure of Canadian constitutional analysis. Like many modern constitutions, Canada's Charter enumerates rights and contains a general limitations clause saying that almost all of those rights are subject to "such reasonable limitations as are demonstrably justified in a free and democratic society", language with roots in the Universal Declaration of Human

Rights. The general limitations clause has been interpreted to impose a standard of proportionality.[11] Suppose, then, that the Canadian Supreme Court finds a statute inconsistent with the Charter because the Court believes that the statute fails the proportionality requirement on the ground that there are less restrictive methods of achieving the state's goals.[12] The legislature can respond with evidence supporting its conclusion that there is in fact no less restrictive method. That would lead to step 5, in which the court would decide whether the legislature's response is adequate.

The interaction between courts and legislatures at steps 3 through 5 is dialogic.[13] Dialogic systems have the advantage over more traditional ones of reducing the countermajoritarian difficulty through structural means. They do so by acknowledging the fact of reasonable disagreement over the *specification* (or concretization, as it is sometimes called) of abstractly described constitutional terms. Consider the example of a guarantee of human dignity or freedom of expression. Often people equally committed to those values will disagree about what they mean in specific contexts. A good example is provided by hate speech regulations, which implicate constitutional guarantees of freedom of expression, equality, and human dignity. People equally committed to those guarantees can disagree, and reasonably so, over whether hate speech regulation in general, or particular versions of such regulations, strike a constitutionally acceptable balance of those values.

The countermajoritarian difficulty can now be seen as an institutional version of reasonable disagreement over the proper specification of abstractly defined values. The difficulty is that the court's position on the question of specification, while reasonable, prevails over the legislature's also-reasonable position on that question. (It is enough that the legislature's position be reasonable, not that it be more reasonable – as assessed by whom? – than the court's position.) Dialogic systems of review make it possible for the legislature to reassess its position in light of what the court has said. Perhaps the legislature

---

11 Nothing important to the present analysis turns on the fact that Canada uses a general limitations clause rather than a series of rights-specific limitations clauses.

12 For a discussion of proportionality, see Chapter 4.

13 Other examples include the Human Rights Act 1998 in the United Kingdom, which authorizes high courts to issue a declaration that a statute is incompatible with certain rights and the New Zealand Bill of Rights Act, which directs courts to interpret statutes to conform to fundamental rights even if doing so distorts somewhat the conclusion a court would reach using ordinary methods of constitutional interpretation.

will be persuaded that the court's position is better reasoned than its own earlier one, and will do nothing. But, after considering the court's position, the legislature might continue to hold the view that its initial position was reasonable enough. If so, the legislature can make it the governing rule.

A dialogue might be fruitful in several situations (Dixon 2008). First, the *outdated* statute: A statute remains on the books years after its enactment, but perhaps lacks significant current support. Its continued existence and sporadic enforcement work harm to a few people, but not many. As a result, repealing the statute is not a legislative priority, or in Dixon's terms, those harmed by the statute have a burden of overcoming legislative inertia. The court can invalidate the statute. The legislature can then re-enact it if the court's implicit evaluation of contemporary values is mistaken and the statute actually retains sufficient public support. Dialogic review shifts the burden of legislative inertia, a not insignificant fact, but does not necessarily displace legislation that has sufficient contemporary public support.

Second, *unconstitutional details*: As noted in the discussion of political constitutionalism, complex legislation with many details may contain obscure provisions that on their own might be thought unconstitutional, and sometimes two or more details will interact in ways that produce unconstitutional results. The legislature might have overlooked the details when enacting the larger statute, or might have failed to understand the interaction. The court can point out the constitutional problem, saying that those details could be altered without impairing the statute's effectiveness. The legislature can then respond. The British experience suggests that quite often the legislature will agree that it had not considered the problem and that repairing the statute to eliminate the constitutional difficulty is relatively easy. But that might not always be the case. The legislature might respond that tinkering with these details will cause numerous complications in how the statute operates as a whole, which the court did not understand. It will then leave the statute unchanged. Or, perhaps more interestingly, the provision might have been fully considered because it was important in assembling the political coalition that supported the larger legislation. Altering the provision would disrupt the political equilibrium reached at the time of initial enactment. Note here that the precise form of dialogic review might matter in the case of the unconstitutional detail resulting from coalition bargaining: The passage of time might make it impossible to reassemble the enacting coalition to re-enact the statute with an override clause but also might make it impossible to assemble a coalition to respond to a mere declaration of incompatibility. A Canadian-style system of dialogic review would leave the court with the last word in this situation, whereas a British-style system would leave the last word to the enacting legislature.

Coalition bargaining leads to a third possibility: a generalization of the "outdated statute" example because the statute actually lacks "true" majority support even at the moment of enactment. In this scenario the statute is enacted because of bargaining within the governing coalition. A small but important part of the governing coalition strongly desires the statute; the rest of the coalition is moderately opposed to the statute but needs the intense minority's support to enact the rest of its program; the intense minority makes enactment of the statute a condition of its support for the rest of the coalition's program; and the opposition is strongly opposed to the statute. A judicial invalidation of the statute might have substantial public support, and – the rest of the coalition's program having been enacted – the intense minority might no longer have the bargaining power to insist on its re-enactment.[14]

Depending on circumstances a dialogic system's advantages are realized when the court's interpretation of the constitution holds *and* when it does not. The disadvantage of dialogic systems is that they assume good faith on everyone's part but, in particular, good faith on the part of the legislature. That is, they work well only if the legislature takes seriously its responsibility for adhering to the constitution and listens to the courts when they raise constitutional objections to statutes the legislature has enacted.[15] Dialogic systems will not work well if the legislature *regularly* disregards the court's actions. (Note, however, that "disregard" might not be an appropriate term when the court's action is accompanied by a reasoned dissent, with which the legislature agrees.) Regular disregard may do no more than convert a system nominally authorizing constitutional review of legislation into a system of parliamentary supremacy. But here form may matter: Systems of parliamentary supremacy are consistent with constitutionalism when, and because, the legislature regularly considers constitutional ques-

---

14 This is a stylized version of the role religious parties have played in much of Israel's constitutional history.

15 The most substantial analysis of this issue is contained in work in progress by Scott Stephenson, an initial version of which was presented at the American Society of Comparative Law, Younger Comparativists Conference, April 2013.

tions in enacting statutes. A legislature that regularly disregards reasoned judicial judgments on constitutional issues is unlikely to be constitutionally responsible in the sense needed to justify parliamentary supremacy.

With the basics of dialogic systems in hand, we can consider several additional matters. Dialogic review operates over a relatively short time period – enactment, constitutional review, and an immediate opportunity for legislative response – and is most suitable when the legislature and executive lack a majority to amend the constitution in response to a court decision. The possibility of amendment and the time period are important aspects of the structure of dialogic review.

Dialogic review and easy amendment rules are partial substitutes. That is, if it is easy to amend the constitution – in the extreme, by a qualified majority in a single legislative setting (rather than by a majority of a quorum, as for ordinary legislation) – decisions by the constitutional court can be final and absolute without enabling anything close to judicial supremacy or a serious countermajoritarian difficulty. At the same time, of course, easy amendment rules substantially reduce the advantages that attend the existence of constitutional review itself.

Dialogic review can be contrasted with another form of constitutional dialogue occurring over a more extended period. The political scientist Robert Dahl observed of the US Supreme Court that the Supreme Court's actions over a reasonably extended time period were rarely out of line with the policy views of the then-governing political coalition (Dahl 1957). The structural reason for this is clear. If the political branches have significant input into the selection of constitutional court judges, and if there is in fact a dominant political coalition for an extended time period, the ordinary processes of retirement, resignation, and death of constitutional court justices will give the dominant coalition the opportunity to fill the constitutional court with judges broadly sympathetic to its positions.

The two conditions in the preceding formulation are important. Recalling a Kelsenian theme: The process for selecting constitutional court judges must have significant political input. Many modern systems of selecting constitutional court judges have sought to *reduce* input from the political branches. These systems use judicial selection commissions with representation from the judiciary, from civil society, and from the government, raising the possibility – which has been realized in some places – that the government's input will be quite weak. We can expect significant tension between the constitutional court and the government under such circumstances.[16]

Tension is particularly likely if the second condition, that there be a governing coalition in power over a relatively extended period, is met. If there is a regular swing between one governing coalition to another quite different coalition, or if government is divided, with one party controlling the executive and another the legislature, the constitutional court will have space to operate relatively free from political constraint. Contrary to Dahl's perception, there will be no long-term dialogue because the court will not have a single partner with whom it can engage in dialogue. Or, perhaps more precisely, as noted earlier whatever the constitutional court does will have support from one of the other institutions of government – the president or the legislature, or the majority coalition or the opposition coalition that has a real possibility of occupying office in the short run.

So far we have considered the relation between structures of constitutional review and political coalitions where the coalitions lack the numbers to amend the constitution. There is a final category worth noting: Structures of constitutional review in dominant-party systems, defined as those in which a single party or coalition holds power for an extended period and has enough votes to amend the constitution. Constitutional review is likely to play a small but sometimes significant role in dominant-party systems.

Constitutional court judges in such systems are likely to have relatively little true independence. They will be chosen by the dominant party and are likely to share the views associated with that party. Any constitutional decisions they make can be overturned easily if they are inconsistent with what the dominant party prefers. Put another way, constitutional review in dominant party systems is unlikely to be counter-"majoritarian" in effect (the scare quotes indicating that the dominant party might not represent a true majority). Perhaps the judges' interest in assisting in good governance might lead them to engage in subconstitutional review, such as enforcing rules allocating

---

16 India provides an example of a system in which the judiciary itself has in practice assumed responsibility for appointing judges in the highest court, though various norms governing the choice of individuals – dealing with their age at appointment coupled with a mandatory retirement age – have reduced the possibility of long-term tension.

authority to specific institutions, subject to easy reconsideration by the dominant party (Yap 2013). Occasional exercises of truly constitutional review might have effects similar to those of dialogic review, prompting reconsideration of the challenged policy by the dominant party.

Finally, the courts might be instruments of the dominant party. This is a common theme in the literature dealing with the rule of law in authoritarian nations (Ginsburg and Moustafa 2008). A sketch of the role of courts in the People's Republic of China lays out the logic. The Communist Party wants the *lower* courts to be independent of control by local party officials so that the "center" in Beijing can use the courts as a way of learning what is going on outside its immediate sphere of control, so as to impose discipline on rogue party officials in the provinces. The lower courts are independent in some sense, but only as long as, and to the extent that, the dominant party sees some advantages in having independent courts. Should the independent courts contravene the dominant party's positions on important matters, the dominant party is likely to respond by checking the courts' power. That, in turn, will reduce the courts' independence overall, and deny the dominant party some of the advantages it gets from having independent courts. So the dominant party's leaders might make a strategic calculation that the benefits they get from having independent courts are large enough to outweigh the occasional setback they face on specific matters.

3.6 The relation between structures of constitutional review and second- and third-generation constitutional rights

Modern constitutions embody classical first-generation rights related to political and civic freedom and to equality and second-generation rights related to social and economic well-being. They increasingly embody third-generation rights to culture, language, and the environment as well. Questions about the judicial enforceability of second-generation rights were raised for several decades, but today the issue is less whether courts should enforce such rights and is rather how they should do so.

Courts typically enforce classical first-generation rights through coercive orders directing that government officials take action to ensure that the rights are honored: They must release a defendant from prison if the substantive law under which the defendant was convicted violated constitutional rights or if the procedures used to convict did so; they must eliminate inequalities by ensuring that burdens or benefits are distributed equally.[17]

Courts and scholars have been skeptical about the availability of equally coercive remedies for violations of second-generation rights. As suggested by the discussion in Chapter 2, sometimes the skepticism was rooted in constitutional texts that described those rights as "directive principles of public policy" and the like, terms not used in connection with first-generation rights. Such textual formulations gradually disappeared, and even courts in countries whose constitutions retained that language were creative in finding second-generation rights embedded in textual provisions other than the directive principles. India provides the clearest example. There the Supreme Court located second-generation rights in a judicial-enforceable "right to life", on the theory, roughly, that second-generation rights to food and shelter were essential components of the right to (a dignified human) life.

With the textual issues put aside, questions about coercive enforcement took a different form. Acknowledging that coercive enforcement of first-generation rights was costly – whether through direct outlays or through increased risks of socially undesirable conduct – critics of coercive enforcement of second-generation rights argued that such enforcement was significantly and systematically *more* expensive than enforcement of first-generation rights. Sometimes this objection was phrased in terms of the separation of powers between the legislature and the courts. Determining the state budget was quintessentially a task for the legislature and the executive. Yet, coercive enforcement of second-generation rights would have significant effects on both the size and the distribution of the budget, intruding on legislative prerogatives in a way different from coercive enforcement of first-generation rights. (It is worth noting here that the general countermajoritarian difficulty can also be phrased as a problem of separation of powers, but the budgetary issues associated with second-generation rights

---

17 The remedy for equality violations can be "reading up" a statute by making a benefit available to one group available to others, or by "reading down" the statute by depriving the first group of the statutory benefit. Formally, the choice between reading up and reading down turns on an assessment of the likely legislative preference in light of the court's decision that unequal distribution is constitutionally impermissible.

seemed to skeptics a difference that rendered the usual responses to the countermajoritarian difficulty less effective in this setting.)

As courts began to enforce second-generation rights, however, the questions became more refined. Two main candidates for enforcement mechanisms emerged: *individual-level* remedies and *systemic* remedies. Individual-level remedies are similar to the coercive remedies used to enforce first-generation rights: Having found that an individual has been deprived of a right to shelter or medication, the court orders that appropriate shelter or medication be given to that person. Experience, particularly in Latin American cases dealing with a right to medications, has revealed serious difficulties associated with individual-level remedies. First, when ordered on a large scale individual-level remedies create serious problems in administering a socially sensible program dealing with the specific right at issue. The difficulty is not that these remedies are costly, but that they are ordered almost randomly. No individual judge or even a high court can take a synoptic view of all the cases to see if the right is being allocated in a socially sensible way – if, for example, the "right" people are receiving the right to shelter or to medication, where "rightness" is determined according to some socially rational plan. Second, and related, the distribution of the right is not entirely random. It depends on which individuals get to court, and experience suggests, albeit not conclusively, that people with reasonable amounts of resources – the "middle classes", roughly – are better able to invoke the courts' powers than the truly poor (Landau 2012). Third, courts appear to be unable to use individual-level remedies with respect to violations of *one* second-generation right in ways that coordinate the provision of that right with the provision of *other* second-generation rights: Cases involving a right to medication are handled quite separately from cases involving a right to shelter, even though good social planning would try to coordinate the solution to both problems.

Finally, sometimes the problems manifested in individual cases arise from some systemic problem that is difficult to detect, as one after another case comes to court. The example most widely used today comes from Brazilian right-to-medication cases, where plaintiffs were denied access to low-cost and potentially beneficial medications in some measure because ministries of health were not updating their lists of approved medications quickly enough. Under the pressure of the irrationalities created by individual-level remedies, the health ministries did eventually redesign their systems for updating the lists of approved medications.

This last point suggests that it might be better to develop systemic remedies from the outset. That is, instead of issuing individual-level remedies and hoping that the health ministries will determine why they are losing the cases, the court in a right-to-medication case would tell the health ministries to redesign their system for updating their lists. For this to be truly distinctive from individual-level remedies, the court would sometimes have to deny an individual-level remedy to the party who brought the lawsuit, as happened in one of the leading cases on judicial remedies for violations of second-generation rights.[18]

Systemic remedies have several characteristics. They typically involve intervening in the ordinary operations of complex bureaucracies. Such interventions make high informational demands on judges, who must learn how those bureaucracies operate before they can design effective systemic remedies. Some of that information can be supplied in the initial litigation, at least if the claimant has sufficient resources. For this reason, systemic remedies are likely to be more effective the more resources the claimant has, which can occur through an expansion of the litigation structure that draws in NGOs and representatives not merely of the legislature but of the bureaucracy itself (Epp 1998).

More important, however, is the possibility that the information can be revealed iteratively. The judge makes an initial effort to intervene in the bureaucracy's operation based on the judge's best current understanding of how the bureaucracy operates. Then the judge observes how the initial intervention works in practice, and can "tweak" or alter the remedy in light of experience. This process can recur many times before the court settles on a single, "final" systemic remedy.[19] Note now that dialogic review involves similar iterative processes. Perhaps, then, newly developed dialogic forms of review are especially well suited to the enforcement of relatively newly developed second-generation rights.

---

18 *Government of South Africa v. Grootboom* 2001 (1) SA 46 (CC), probably the leading case on judicial enforcement of social and economic rights; Mrs. Grootboom died before receiving housing provided by a government program.

19 There are some design issues at this stage as well. In particular, the judge can require that plaintiffs monitor the bureaucracy's behavior and revive the litigation if problems persist, or the judge can order the bureaucracy to report periodically on what has occurred.

3.7   The structure of constitutional review and third-generation rights

The enforcement of third-generation rights raises another set of questions, though answers must be quite tentative because there is as yet relatively little experience in enforcing such rights. Third-generation rights are distinguished from first- and second-generation rights because they are *essentially* rights that inhere in groups rather than individuals. Sometimes, of course, denying a third-generation right can generate a harm to an individual, as when a member of a linguistic minority is denied the opportunity to interact with government agencies in his or her own language. But the essence of third-generation rights is that they are provided because groups of people share a common language or a common culture. Consider, for example, a third-generation right to the intellectual property of an indigenous culture, such as its knowledge of the remedial properties of specific plants. Uncompensated commercial exploitation of that right harms the indigenous culture as a whole, not any individual member of the culture.

For structures of constitutional review, the main implication of that understanding of third-generation rights centers on the question of who gets to represent the group. Consider this example: A development initiative threatens the habitat of indigenous people. Some of the indigenous people claim that the initiative will destroy a long-standing farming culture, or make it impossible to continue a form of worship that is intrinsically tied to some landmark that the development project will destroy. Others, however, might find the economic benefits to the group more valuable than preservation of the existing culture. They may note as well that the culture has already undergone some changes as a result of its encounters with the new majority culture, and indeed that change is as much a feature of culture as stasis. Who from within the culture has standing to assert "the culture's" constitutionally protected rights? And, if everyone does, how can constitutional courts be expected to deal with these issues in a sensible way?

The obvious answer is some representative of the indigenous or cultural group or some representative of the ecosystem. Yet, there might be conflicts within the group, with some believing that the best thing for the group would be to build the development and adjust cultural practices in response, others believing that building the development would eventually destroy the indigenous culture.

The problem of intra-group conflict has been most discussed in connection with conflicts between traditional cultural practices and the requirement that women be treated equally with men. Saying that a traditional group's traditional leaders have some privileged position in identifying aspects of group culture threatened by some legislative provision may under-value the fact – if it is a fact – that the group's culture is always being negotiated and changed in response to changes in the group's social and, importantly, legal environment. Conceptually, we might allow anyone embedded in the culture to make claims about what that culture "is" or is becoming. Implementing such a position in real institutions is likely to be quite difficult. Some in the culture might have greater access to resources, for example. Others might be able to call on sympathetic outsiders to counter the resource imbalance, but doing so raises questions about the extent to which the outsiders – typically, NGOs – can truly identify values within the culture.

One solution is to open the litigation structure quite widely, allowing everyone who can plausibly claim to represent "the group" to present relevant arguments. Another solution is to have some general designation of a group representative – an NGO or a public "defender" of the group – and then allow those within the group who disagree with the position taken by that entity to intervene. With the latter, one might want to worry about the possibility that the courts will give special weight to the position presented by the designated entity. One way of addressing that concern is to examine the decision-making process that led the entity to take the position it did: How widely did it consult before taking the position? How many staff positions in the entity are filled by members of the group on whose behalf they are said to speak?

Students of indigenous cultures have shown that these cultures are often, and perhaps always, created and sustained by law external to them. Absent external legal regulation, the boundaries of any culture – and so the content of any cultural right – are fluid. The structure of representation in connection with constitutional review of third-generation rights may then be understood as the version of the legal construction of culture specific to constitutional review.

These problems recur in a slightly different form in connection with environmental rights. Constitutional provisions for environmental rights already provide the basis for distinguishing between rights *of* the environment itself and rights of humans *in* the environment (Cho and Pedersen 2013). Conceptualizing the latter may not pose major difficulties: Humans can assert that some development project that threatens a habitat with distinctive flora and fauna poses a risk that humans will be deprived of some as-yet-undiscovered compounds that might have valuable pharmaceutical advantages. And courts might be able to assess the balance between the economic and other benefits of development and the risk (or uncertainty) in connection with these potential losses to humans from the loss of biodiversity.

Rights of the environment itself are simultaneously more profound and more difficult to implement. A classic article in the literature of US environmental law made the central point – which again can be described as one of standing, but now in a truly deep sense – by referring to the song "Ol' Man River" from the musical *Showboat* (Sagoff 1974). That song's lyrics include the lines: "'Ol' man river ... mus' know something ... But ol' man river, he jes keeps rollin' along". Sagoff asks us to imagine a proposal to erect a dam on the river that would support a large-scale electrical supply to the region and, of course, stop the river from simply rolling along. What are the river's rights as a river – to keep on rolling or to provide humans with energy? Environmental philosophers may have begun to sketch the contours of a right in the environment as such, but legal scholars have done almost nothing to translate such a right into terms suitable for use in a legal system.

3.8   Conclusion

The classic issues in comparative constitutional design of the choice between centralized and dispersed judicial review, and between specialized and centralized constitutional courts, have taken on new baggage over the past generation. More, the development of dialogic forms of constitutional review interacts interestingly with the development of enforceable social and economic rights. As third-generation rights gain more prominence, we will undoubtedly discover further connections between those rights and structures of constitutional review, or see additional innovations in forms of constitutional review. All these provide arenas for scholarly inquiry over the next decade.

4 The structure of rights analysis: proportionality, rules and international law

4.1 Introduction

Every student of comparative constitutional law will compare the ways in which specific rights are protected (or not) in national constitutions. It is unlikely that any generalization about rights-protection will withstand scrutiny. Rights-protection appears to be an area in which national histories and experiences shape constitutional law. The United States is almost unique in guaranteeing an individual right to possess weapons, for example. How can we think about that fact? One possibility is to generate the right from a general account of the prerequisites of constitutionalism itself: a citizenry with the physical capacity to stand up to domestic tyrants. Yet, the near uniqueness of the US provision suggests that such a general account will be insufficient, for why have few other national constitutions perceived the same need for such a right to serve the same purpose? Rather, a better explanation almost certainly lies in central aspects of US culture – the experience, actual at one point, imagined today, of moving to a dangerous frontier, for example (Tushnet 2007).

It might be worth a moment to generate similar examples where variations in rights-protection are probably best attributed to national histories and experiences. Constitutional doctrine in the United States is hostile to regulation of hate speech, whereas such regulation is elsewhere widely thought to be consistent with constitutional guarantees of free expression. The difference probably lies in experiences outside the United States in which hate speech or its analogues appears to have played a significant role in producing gross and relatively recent violations of human rights. Supporters of French regulations severely limiting a woman's right to cover her face in public for religious reasons sometimes cite the French traditions of equality and fraternity, which are said to require, on the French understanding, open face-to-face interactions among equal citizens (Zoller 2010). Lacking such a tradition, other nations might find such bans inconsistent with their understanding of religious liberty.

These examples are of course mere sketches, precisely because the culturalist approach to rights-protections can be implemented in its most persuasive form only through quite detailed examinations of nationally specific events and understandings. For that reason, this chapter forgoes inquiry into the specifics of rights-protection. Instead, it focuses on the general structure of rights-protection and specifically, on the argument that the doctrine of proportionality provides the best method for analyzing whether some government action violates a constitutional right (without regard to the specific content of the right). Proponents of proportionality analysis differ among themselves on matters of detail, but the structure of the arguments is sufficiently similar to make "proportionality" itself the object of inquiry. In examining proportionality, this chapter contrasts proportionality analysis with a reasonably close cousin, "balancing" and with the major intellectual competitor to proportionality analysis, the use of relatively categorical rules to determine whether constitutional rights have been violated. (For general descriptions and defenses of proportionality analysis, see Beatty 2004 and Barak 2012.)

4.2   Balancing, proportionality and rules compared

The background against which discussions of the three approaches to determining whether constitutional rights have been violated occurs is a strong presumption of constitutionality. This can be characterized as itself a rule – against finding statutes unconstitutional except in the most extreme cases. Once a constitutional court abjures a strong presumption of constitutionality, it must decide how to determine when a challenged action is unconstitutional.

Balancing is a technique in which the court describes all the considerations at stake – the governmental interest the challenged regulation serves, the impairment of constitutional values and more, all with appreciation for the fact that interests and impairments and everything else come in degrees. Having in mind all these considerations, a balancing court decides what outcome is best from the court's own point of view, all things considered. The court's point of view is determined by the values the court's members hold. These values can be substantive – about the importance of national security or free expression; they can be institutional, based on a judge's view of the proper relation between courts and legislatures; and indeed they can range widely across the entire domain of value. The central point is that the "all things considered" judgment is made from the court's point of view, not that of the legislature or the ordinary citizen, or any other candidate one might proffer.

A balancing approach can be qualified by institutional considerations. Specifically, a balancing court can give some degree of deference to legislative judgments (or judgments by other decision-makers such as executive officials or administrators) of a certain sort: judgments on matters about which legislatures (or the other decision-makers) are likely to have more expertise than the judges, and in cases where the legislature is likely to deploy its expertise rather than use it as a façade behind which "pure" value judgments are being made.

The core idea of proportionality analysis is that it provides a structured form of analysis. Consider a statute challenged as unconstitutional.[1] Proportionality analysis begins by asking whether the goal the government seeks to advance through the statute is a permissible one. A statute that does an exceptionally good job of promoting torture, or of promoting racial segregation for its own sake, would fail at this stage. It may be worth noting that courts engaging in proportionality analysis cannot compile too large a list of impermissible purposes, because doing so would threaten to collapse the entire analysis into the first step: A rights-violation would be defined as one pursuing an impermissible purpose (of violating one of a large list of purposes said to be impermissible because they seek to violate one or another right).

Next, the analysis asks whether the statute infringes – that is, has some adverse effect upon – a person's ability to exercise a constitutionally protected right. Many courts tend to take the position that liberal constitutions guarantee a general right to liberty, that is, a right to do whatever one wants unless some law prohibits the action. If there is such a general right to liberty, it will be the rare statute that does not infringe that or some other right. It may be important here to emphasize a difference in terminology between proportionality analysis and rule-based analysis: In proportionality analysis, the term "infringement" refers to any adverse effect on liberty, whereas in rules-based discourse the term tends to state a conclusion that the statute violates the constitution.

---

1   The following discussion omits consideration of some important issues, such as which party bears the burden of persuasion with respect to various components of the analysis.

After finding an infringement, proportionality analysis asks whether a reasonable person could reasonably believe that the statute would do *something* – not much perhaps, but something – to advance the government's permissible goal. (This is sometimes described as a "minimal rationality" requirement.) Next, the analysis asks whether the government's goals could be advanced at least as well by some other means that has a smaller adverse effect on liberty. This is a "minimal impairment" or "least restrictive means" requirement. Finally, if the statute survives all the prior stages of analysis, the inquiry turns to proportionality "as such", that is, whether the government's goals are important enough and are advanced enough by the statute so as to justify the actual impairment of liberty.

The difference between proportionality analysis and balancing is reasonably clear: Proportionality analysis has a structure that balancing lacks. In contrast, it takes some care to specify the precise difference between proportionality analysis and a rule-based analysis. Obviously, any particular result reached by proportionality analysis can be reached by a well-formulated rule (simply build into the rule the considerations used in the proportionality analysis). And, though I do not know of any analysis that establishes the following, I think it also correct that proportionality analysis and a rules-based analysis can be what philosophers might call extensionally equivalent. That is, take any collection of results reached through proportionality analysis and it will be possible to develop an internally consistent set of rules (with qualifications, exceptions with specified domains of application and so on) that produces the same results.[2]

Yet, if the modes of analysis do not necessarily produce different results, in what sense are they truly different? Proponents of proportionality analysis suggest that it is better than both balancing and a rules-based analysis because it is more objective, simpler and more transparent. Notably, some of the criticisms of proportionality analysis suggest that it is inferior to balancing along some dimensions and inferior to rule-based decision-making along other dimensions. Even if the criticisms are accurate, then, proportionality analysis may be the "least bad" overall of the three approaches.

---

2 Extensional equivalence would also require that, when we add some new result from proportionality analysis, it will be possible to reorganize and supplement the rule-system so that it retains internal consistency and produces the same new result.

4.2.1 Objectivity

Here the primary contrast is between proportionality analysis and generalized balancing. Balancing tests direct judges to consider all the relevant features of a problem and then to determine whether on balance the challenged statute is constitutional. Critics of balancing from both a proportionality perspective and a rules perspective argue that balancing is simply too open-ended. What is a "relevant" feature of a problem will change from case to case even within a defined doctrinal field such as free expression, and judges can proliferate such considerations at will, or arbitrarily truncate their analysis, in the service of some ideological or party-political position. The several-step structure of proportionality analysis is said to constrain judges more effectively than a balancing approach will.

The claim that proportionality analysis is more objective than balancing is open to question. Consider a simple example involving the "least restrictive alternative" step. In that step the court asks whether the government could accomplish its goals equally well but without infringing on the protected right as much, through some alternative means. If asked honestly, that question should almost always receive the answer "No". An example that illustrates the general point is this: The government requires all homeowners to separate their trash into recyclable and non-recyclable bins, charging them a fee for the two bins. A homeowner objects, asserting that she is a good steward of the planet who rarely uses non-recyclable materials and that when she does, her neighbors are happy to place her trash with theirs. She argues that it is unfair – a denial of her right to liberty, perhaps – to make her buy the bin for non-recyclable materials because, she points out, she is not contributing to ecological degradation. There is a less restrictive alternative to the "bin buying" requirement: Grant an exemption to everyone who shows that they generate little non-recyclable trash and that they have alternative, equally effective ways of disposing of it. The government responds that the proposed alternative is not really one that would achieve equivalent results with a smaller impairment of liberty, because setting up and then using a system to determine who should get an exemption will itself raise the cost of the government's program.

Putting the foregoing point in the most general terms, the government seeks to advance various substantive goals at a cost it finds acceptable. Rarely will there be another means that achieves the substantive goal at the same (or lower) cost (Note Robert Nagel] 1972). So, any alternative means that achieves the same level with respect to the substantive goal will almost always be more expensive. One response to this difficulty might be to elaborate the "minimal impairment" requirement to incorporate some sensitivity to the degree of intrusion on constitutionally protected interests: The more substantial the impairment, the less weight administrative and similar concerns should have. The modified version might actually exacerbate the underlying difficulty. When a court finds a statute unconstitutional at the "least restrictive alternative" or "minimal impairment" stage, it is making a value judgment about the relative importance of cost-savings on the margin and liberty-protection on the margin.[3] That is not the objectivity claimed for proportionality analysis.

Obviously, the same problem affects the stage at which the court evaluates proportionality as such. For, at that stage, the court openly reaches its own judgment about the relative importance of the incremental gains to policy and the incremental harms to liberty. Some advocates of proportionality analysis have tried to cabin the discretion associated with proportionality as such. Robert Alexy, for example, argues that we can achieve general agreement in almost all cases on a rough judgment that the harms to liberty are minor, intermediate, or serious, and can do the same with respect to the gains to the government's policy goals (Alexy 2002). Then, he argues, cases that fall into the "high-low" categories – serious incursion on liberty with modest gains to policy, or minor incursions on liberty with substantial gains to policy – can be resolved easily.

Whether this strategy substantially allays concern that courts using proportionality analysis make their own, independent judgments about rights and policy depends on a number of factors:

(1)   Probably the most important factor is the contention that most cases can be resolved before the stage of proportionality as such, and the concern about objectivity actually arises in only a handful of cases. It does seem to be the case that courts committed to proportionality analysis dispose of the large bulk of their cases at the earlier stages in the analysis, and are especially attracted to

---

3 Nothing in the general analysis turns on the example of administrative expense. The analysis requires only that the regulation's primary goal be accompanied, as it almost inevitably will be, by some additional goal or goals.

finding statutes unconstitutional at the "minimal impairment" stage. Still, disposing of cases at that stage does not really eliminate the concern about objectivity.

(2)   How many cases actually fall into the "high-low" categories? If the answer is that relatively few do, proportionality as such is not systemically substantially more objective than balancing.

(3)   How often will there actually be general agreement that a problem has the relevant "high, intermediate, or low" characteristics? One might worry about the possibility that describing the characteristics is itself a (discretionary) choice. This worry might be exacerbated by the observation that a legislature, knowing that its output is subject to proportionality analysis of this sort, might have reached a different judgment about the problem's characteristics. That is, what the court describes as a statute that promotes the legislative goals to an intermediate extent, might have been regarded by the legislature as one that promoted that goal to a high level. Note too that this difficulty is enhanced when we understand the point made earlier, that legislatures have complex goals. A defender of proportionality analysis might respond by referring to the realities of the legislative process, contending that legislatures rarely do much in the way of assessing incremental contributions to policy or harms to liberty. The critic might reply in turn that the proportionality analysis being described is one in which quite rough categorical judgments are made and that legislatures actually do make such judgments even if they do not engage in close and careful analysis of marginal benefits and harms. And, as we will see, constitutional review can be structured to encourage legislatures to engage in the right kind of assessment.

(4)   What are courts to do with cases that do not fall within the "high-low" categories? One possibility is that they can preserve objectivity by rejecting constitutional challenges whenever a case falls outside those categories. Here proportionality analysis might almost reduce to a rule-like analysis, with a large swathe of cases subject to what amounts to a strong presumption of constitutionality.

(5)   Finally, the strategy of rough categorization reduces another of the benefits claimed for proportionality analysis – its transparency. Describing a statute as making a modest contribution to the government's policy goals may be less transparent than the more discursive description of the statute's effects associated with pure balancing approaches.

4.2.2   Simplicity

Proportionality analysis is said to be simpler than balancing and is an analytic approach that is intuitively appealing, with strong parallels to the way ordinary people make daily decisions. But, of course, rules have the virtue of simplicity too – and indeed, a stripped-down rule-system that provides "simple rules for a complex world" (Epstein 1995) can be simpler than any proportionality analysis.

Yet, at least in many domains of constitutional law stripped-down rule-systems are difficult to develop and sustain. The general problem is straightforward. Begin with a simple rule and you will find, typically relatively soon, a case whose resolution pursuant to that rule seems intuitively wrong. The decision-maker will be tempted to develop an "exception" to the rule that produces the intuitively correct result in the new case while preserving the remainder of the rule for all other cases. The exception can itself be formulated in rule-like terms by identifying the characteristic of the new case that seems to generate the tension with the simple rule, and then describing the exception with reference to that characteristic. But, of course, new cases will continue to arise and applying the rule and its exception will sometimes, once again, seem to generate an intuitively unattractive result. So, the decision-maker generates an exception to the exception, or a qualification to the rule, or a new exception. In the end, the rule-system is no longer simple.

(It is worth noting that the "rule plus numerous exceptions" structure can be described differently – as identifying the boundaries of the protected right. If we think of the protected right as a territory and the rule as identifying subdomains into which the government's regulatory power cannot reach, the exceptions carve notches around the edges of those domains where the government can regulate.)

Consider an example drawn from the contemporary US law of free expression, typically described as quintessentially rule-based and (sometimes) offered as an example of why rules are better than proportionality. Mitchell Berman (2010) offers what he describes as a simplified version of the US law of freedom of expression:

> A law constitutes an impermissible abridgment of the freedom of speech if: it regulates expression on the basis of its content or viewpoint and is not narrowly tailored to achieve a compelling governmental interest, except

that content-based regulation of non-misleading speech that proposes a lawful economic transaction is permitted if the regulation directly advances a substantial government interest that could not be advanced equally well by a less speech-restrictive regulation, and except too that content-based regulation of speech is freely permitted if, inter alia, the regulated speech proposes an unlawful economic transaction or a lawful transaction in a misleading way, or if it is sexually explicit and as a whole appeals to the prurient interest, and depicts or describes sexual conduct in a patently offensive way, and lacks serious artistic, political, or scientific value, or if it includes the sexually explicit depiction of children, or if the speech, by its very utterance inflicts injury or tends to incite an immediate breach of the peace; all subject to the caveat that even when speech may permissibly be regulated, if that regulation takes the form of a prior restraint on its issuance, then the regulation is ordinarily presumptively impermissible; and furthermore, a content-neutral regulation of speech is impermissible unless it is narrowly tailored to achieve a significant government interest and leaves open ample alternative channels of communication.

And, this is only the beginning. For example, sometimes a content-based regulation will be permissible if the regulated speech has "secondary effects" and content-based regulations of "true threats" are constitutionally permissible.

Perhaps, though, the US rule-system has become undesirably complex and could be simplified to restore its advantage over proportionality. Simplification comes at a cost, though – the generation of results that are intuitively unappealing on the merits. So, for example, explicitly citing the desirability of a simple rule-system, the US Supreme Court has held it unconstitutional for a legislature to ban films and videos showing exceptionally violent treatment of animals and to make it a crime deliberately to lie about having received a medal for military service.[4] In neither case did the Court assert that the regulated materials made a significant contribution to public discourse or otherwise advanced the interests served by a system of free expression. Rather, the Court said that developing a (new) exception for these cases, so as to reach a substantively appealing result, would weaken the overall rule-like structure of free speech analysis.

Perhaps so, in the abstract, but given the existing complexity of the rule-system, one can fairly wonder about the size of the incremental

---

4 *United States v. Stevens*, 559 US 460 (2010); *United States v. Alvarez*, 567 US --- (2012).

weakening of the already complex structure. Put another way, one might fairly ask, "Given that the courts have already developed such a large number of exceptions to a categorical rule against content-based regulation, what reason is there for refusing to develop another exception so as to reach an intuitively appealing result in this case?" At some point – probably at a point well before the US structure took its current shape – the honest answer would be: "There is no reason specific to this case or problem, but we must maintain the rule-system as best we can". That is an almost explicit invocation of arbitrariness, an undesirable characteristic of legal doctrine.[5] Sometimes the US Supreme Court attempts to offer a substantive explanation for its refusal to develop a new exception, but when it does so the purported explanation is typically quite weak. This reduces the transparency of the rule-system.

How do rules and proportionality fare when compared along the dimension of simplicity? In principle, a rule-system can be simpler than proportionality. But in practice, rule-systems are likely to become quite complex, or their simplicity can be sustained only at the cost of arbitrariness or reduction in transparency.

Still, those costs might be defensible on grounds related to the institutional capacity of higher courts. The general form of the defense is relatively simple, though working out its details can be quite complex. We can call the argument an "institutional risk of error" analysis.

The argument begins with the perspective of the higher court. Its judges have a set of substantive views about what results are correct in a range of cases. (These were described above as the "intuitively appealing" results.) We can assume that proportionality analysis provides the best account of how these judges generate the set of correct results. That is, given a problem, they ask themselves, "Is the proposed solution proportional in the constitutional sense?" The correct results are those that are indeed proportional.

The judges want to maximize the chances that the overall system of legislation and adjudication generates as many of these correct results

---

5 As developed below, an "institutional risk of error" analysis might explain why a court might forgo offering a reasoned explanation for refusing to create a new exception or qualification: Doing so would make that reason available to other decision-makers, such as legislators and lower courts, who might not use it to achieve the results the higher court thinks appropriate.

as possible. If they knew that they could consider every case and every statute, they would adopt proportionality analysis, because doing so generates the correct results every time – again, from their point of view. But, they know that, as a practical matter, they cannot review every case and statute. So, they know that they must develop a way of thinking about when statutes violate the constitution that will generate as many correct results as possible in the *un*reviewed situations. They also know that legislators and judges in lower courts might not share their own judgments about what the correct results are. In short, other decision-makers will make mistakes, as the higher court judges would see them.

For this reason the higher court judges should develop a way of thinking about the constitution that minimizes the risk of error by other decision-makers, not all of whom will share the values or abilities of the higher court judges. From the perspective of higher court judges, both proportionality and generalized balancing might generate "too many" unreviewable errors. The reason is that those analytic approaches leave rather wide room for discretionary decision, as the discussion of the purported objectivity of proportionality showed. So the higher court judges might prefer to develop a system of rules. The rules will tell other decision-makers – and tell them in clear terms – the boundaries of their authority. To do that effectively, however, the rule-system must be relatively simple. Proliferating exceptions and qualifications obscures the message the doctrinal structure is supposed to send. The arbitrariness and loss of transparency that come with the preservation of a simple rule-system are costs worth bearing so that, overall, the legal system maximizes the number of correct results.

The case for rules over proportionality and balancing is not yet complete, however. There is another cost to adherence to rules by the higher court. Doing so requires that the higher court sometimes generates results that, from the point of view of the judges on that very court, are wrong – because, again, introducing complexity sends the wrong message to other decision-makers. Rule-systems generate mistakes at the higher court level, but the tradeoff is that they reduce the number (and importance?) of mistakes made elsewhere, mistakes that cannot be corrected by the higher court because of limits on its capacity.

This "institutional risk of error" analysis does offer an account of the superiority of rule-systems over proportionality. One might be skeptical, however, about its empirical basis. In particular, it requires that judges in the higher court tolerate and even acknowledge that the results in the cases they deal with are sometimes erroneous from their own point of view. This may be a difficult state to sustain psychologically, especially when the alternative – generate a new exception – is so obviously at hand.

4.2.3　Transparency

In one sense rules are necessarily *un*transparent. By adopting a rule a decision-maker screens out of consideration some features of a situation that would rationally be taken into account were the decision-maker to decide on an "all things considered" basis. (The decision-maker might adopt a rule for "institutional risk of error" reasons, or to defer to the judgment of another decision-maker regarded by the rule-adopter as more expert in the field.) The features screened out of consideration disappear from view when the rule is invoked. Sometimes, perhaps, the decision-maker invoking the rule will be compelled to note that the rule has this effect with respect to a specific feature, so then will explain why the feature is being disregarded. In these cases the rule becomes (more) transparent, but – as already suggested – at the cost of complexity.

So, rules almost certainly come up short when compared to proportionality or balancing, to the extent that transparency is desirable. The qualification here may be important. The case for transparency assumes that opacity is a cost. Perhaps it is a cost worth bearing for "institutional risk of error" or other reasons, but it is a cost nonetheless. An alternative view would be that opacity is sometimes a benefit, something that counts in favor of adopting a rule rather than using balancing or proportionality.

The argument is that sometimes society might be better off if decision-makers know that they are actually relying on something that they are not disclosing to their audiences. Guido Calabresi and Philip Bobbitt provided the classic general argument to this effect in describing what they call "tragic choices" (Calabresi and Bobbitt 1978). These are choices to be made in situations where everyone acknowledges that there are important values at stake, and each value is in severe tension with the others. Open discussion of what should be done in such situations might exacerbate rather than resolve disagreement. Calabresi and Bobbitt describe numerous institutional mechanisms for dealing with these situations. All involve some degree of concealment of the fact that the chosen resolution favors one or another of the competing values. For example, relegating the decision to a jury, which renders a binary (guilty or innocent, liable or not liable) and, importantly, unexplained decision, conceals from the parties exactly how the jury weighted the competing values.

Daniel Sabbagh offers affirmative action as an example of the value of opacity in constitutional law (Sabbagh 2007). Simplifying his argument for expository purposes: Affirmative action programs advance important goals, including rectification of past injustice and promotion of racial equality, but are in tension with other important goals, particularly the minimization of the use of racial categories in social decision-making. An opaque policy – one that conceals the use of race in decision-making – might be preferable to a transparent one that makes it obvious that racial categories are decisive in some instances. So, for example, the US doctrine that "full file" review of applications for university seats, where race is said to be a relevant consideration but cannot be the only one, might be better than a quota or set-aside policy that openly reserves seats for identified racial minorities. And this would be true even if, as all administrators of "full file" policies should acknowledge, in some instances race is indeed dispositive when doing a full file review – that is, sometimes a student is admitted (or denied admission) because of his or her race – just as it is dispositive in set-aside systems.

This example shows how opacity might be preferable to transparency. An important feature of the example is that constitutional doctrine permits university decision-makers to use a technique that obscures race's role in admissions decisions. The administrator, like a jury, makes a binary and unexplained decision. That is, it is not an example of how a *judicial* balancing or "all things considered" approach works, because judicial balancing (and proportionality analysis – though somewhat less so because of its use of a structured analysis) involves explaining what the relevant considerations are and the weight given each consideration (including, in the example, explicit discussion of race's role and importance in allowing affirmative action).

Sabbagh's argument shows how opacity might be preferable to transparency, but – because the opacity occurs at the university level rather than the judicial one – does not illustrate how an opaque rule might be preferable to transparent balancing. An example of the latter might be drawn, again, from US constitutional doctrine, here dealing with freedom of expression. Under that doctrine, governments cannot ban sexually explicit material unless it is obscene, a category from which a great deal of sexually explicit material is excluded. This is a rule-like approach. A court evaluating the constitutionality of a ban on some sexually explicit material using the balancing or proportionality alternatives would have to discuss, among other things, the positive value there might be in the dissemination of non-obscene sexually explicit material. That discussion might well be quite awkward. How effectively would judges be able to explain that the dissemination of such material might provoke sexual fantasies that are valuable means for reducing open sexual violence or – even more – that are valuable means for the development of a healthy personality? By adopting the rule, the US courts might hope to avoid that discussion, although of course at a cost – here, the cost of not discussing the contribution that the dissemination of non-obscene sexually explicit material makes to the prevalence of sexual violence and the subordination of women. And even that hope might be false, because the court would have to define what counts as obscene material under its rule and the definition, if done honestly, probably would have to deal with the purported affirmative value of material just outside and just within the borders of the definition.

The two examples, of affirmative action policy and policy involving the dissemination of sexually explicitly material, lay out the form for arguments defending opacity over transparency and so, for arguments for rules over balancing or proportionality. Whether such arguments should carry the day and if so, in what domains, will of course be controversial and further research on the subject of opacity's value seems warranted.

4.3   Explaining the difference

Differences in national histories, institutions and legal cultures often provide the best explanation for differences in national substantive doctrines. Such differences seem rather less likely to play a part in explaining why proportionality analysis is so widespread and yet underused in the United States, precisely because proportionality analysis is favored in nations with significantly different histories, institutions and legal cultures.

One possible explanation for the difference is simple path-dependence. Once a national legal system starts to use proportionality analysis or a categorical approach, shifting away from it may be difficult. Lawyers' training will be shaped by the approach courts take and their advocacy will in turn reinforce that approach.

Path-dependency might be reinforced by constitutional language, itself perhaps a product of the historical era in which the national constitution was drafted. Modern constitutions contain either general limitations clauses or provision-specific limitations clauses. Syntactically, the *absence* of such clauses in the US Constitution may incline the courts toward adopting a categorical approach. Devising formulas like proportionality to substitute for the categories' boundaries might be thought untethered to text and therefore a license for excessive judicial creativity. This problem would be exacerbated were the US courts to devise a single limitations approach to all the quite different constitutional clauses. The historical point is that the language of limitations clauses derives from post-1945 documents such as the Universal Covenant of Human Rights and the Canadian Charter of Rights. A common origin might conduce to a common interpretive approach.

Closely related to the distinction between proportionality and categorical analysis is a distinction between internal and external limits on constitutional rights. The image here is of a domain of rights. Internal limits define the boundaries of the domain – for example, by defining "the freedom of speech" that is constitutionally protected, and treating everything that lies outside those boundaries as not constitutionally protected at all (that is, the right whose boundaries are under consideration is not protected at all; something outside the boundaries of *that* right might of course be protected by another right). The image of an external limit is of a line cutting across a domain to create something like an arc. Something that falls within the arc is within the domain of the right, but the external limit on the scope of the right provides the justification for permissibly infringing on the right. The boundary-drawing associated with internal limits fits reasonably comfortably with a categorical approach to rights and proportionality might be an apt way of identifying where the external limits cut into the right. In addition, as noted earlier, it is reasonably clear that the boundary-drawing, internal limits approach can be extensionally equivalent to the external, carve-out approach. Finally, in one of the few extended discussions of the contrast between internal and external limits, Robert Alexy argues that the language of the US Constitution strongly suggests that it is best understood as adopting the internal limits approach – and so is conducive to the boundary-drawing, categorical approach – whereas the language of the German Basic Law strongly suggests that it is best understood as adopting the external limits, proportionality approach. The argument, in short, is that constitutional language does indeed account for differences in the structure of constitutional analysis.[6]

Frederick Schauer offered an alternative explanation, confined to the comparison between the categorical US approach to freedom of expression issues and the proportionality approach used elsewhere (Schauer 2005). Schauer argues that the differences arise from the different length of time constitutional courts have had to deal with these issues. The US Supreme Court began to deal with free expression issues seriously toward the end of the First World War and has now accumulated nearly a century's worth of experience in the field. Considering a large number of cases falling within the same general domain, the US Supreme Court has observed that the outcomes in various sets of cases tend to follow a single pattern. So, for example, the results in criminal prosecutions for speech that the government contends will lead to social disorder show that such prosecutions are rarely justified because the government typically exaggerates the threat posed by such speech, and that prosecutions are justified only when the temporal connection between the speech and the ensuing law-violation is quite close. From these results the Court has generated a categorical rule requiring extremely skeptical examination of these cases. And, observing an even wider range of cases, the Court has reached a similar conclusion about any regulation based on the content of speech, with some – again, categorically described – exceptions.

Schauer's argument is that rules precipitate out of extended experience with a set of similar problems. Courts might begin with an unstructured balancing, or even a structured proportionality analysis, but eventually they learn that it is more efficient – and the risk of error is lower – if they formulate and apply categorical rules.

There are several difficulties with Schauer's argument, which, it must be said, can come across as condescending to "younger" constitutional courts. One is analytical. The court must initially classify cases as falling within a defined domain, but nothing inherent in the cases dictates the

---

6 Internal limits might use terms such as "reasonable" that invite proportionality analysis.

classification. In particular, defining the relevant categories as "speech said to be likely to cause social disorder" or "content-based regulations" is a choice made by the court. One might alternatively have defined the first category as "speech critical of government policy", for example. The latter might be seen as an awkward amalgamation of quite different problems – speech said to cause social disorder, for example, and speech said to have the potential to mislead consumers. So, although Schauer might be right in arguing that eventually courts will precipitate rules out of their experience with numerous cases, nothing in his argument tells us which rules will arise.

In addition, Schauer's argument must take into account that the US approach is a rules-plus-exceptions one and sometimes, the exceptions have exceptions themselves. As noted earlier, the more complex the rule structure becomes, the more it resembles either unstructured balancing or structured proportionality approaches. So perhaps US free speech doctrine is on a path that leads from unstructured balancing through categorical rules with numerous exceptions, to the proportionality analysis that other courts have already adopted – perhaps, again, for reasons related to constitutional language.

Another difficulty with Schauer's argument might be called empirical. The US experience with free speech doctrine began in the 1910s and the categorical approach crystallized in the late 1960s and early 1970s – a period of fifty or sixty years. Some other constitutional courts, most notably the German Federal Constitutional Court, operating since 1951, have now had a similar length of experience and yet, they seem not to have abandoned proportionality analysis for categorical rules. This empirical problem is made more acute when we look more discretely at defined domains within free speech law, such as commercial speech. There, the US experience dates from the mid-1970s, contemporaneously with the experience of other constitutional courts with problems in that domain. Again, the United States has a relatively categorical approach to the regulation of commercial speech and other nations do not. Time and experience do not seem sufficient to account for that difference.

An additional feature of Schauer's analysis supports it in one way and undermines it in another. One can begin by asking: Experience with what? Namely, is the relevant domain "freedom of expression overall" or, as the presentation so far has suggested, "freedom of expression in connection with defamation" plus "freedom of information in con-

nection with sedition" plus "commercial speech" and so on. The larger
the domain the wider the range of experience in that domain and
it seems unquestionable that the US Supreme Court has had more
experience over the widest domain than other constitutional courts.
More experience means more information. Perhaps more information
produces better results. And, perhaps, constitutional courts that can
discern which results are better than others, – almost by definition –
would prefer to reach the better results. One might draw an analogy to
scientific progress: More experiments produce more knowledge and
more knowledge leads to better, more scientifically defensible results.[7]

The argument from experience to better results would support
Schauer's argument if progress in law were like progress in science.
Yet, in science we have a metric for determining which results are
better than others: The better results produce better performance in
the world. It is unclear that there is a similar metric for law. The ana-
logue to the metric used for science would be a metric dealing with
something like greater success evaluated according to some pragmatic
judgments. And, we might well have some basis for making such judgments in extreme cases, such as torture. The problems with which
constitutional courts grapple and which Schauer discusses, are typically quite a bit more subtle. Defamation law requires an evaluation
of the comparative value of personal privacy – the damage to personal
life wrought by false statements about one's life – and public information. Each case presents a specific variation on the intrusion on
personal privacy and the benefit to public understanding. Overall, it
seems that European courts tend to place a higher value on privacy and
a lower one on public information than the US Supreme Court does.[8]
Yet, it seems unlikely that one rather than the other evaluation of the
competing values provides better grounds, pragmatically assessed, for
structuring the law of defamation.

(A note on an analogy that might seem initially appealing but is ultimately misleading: The European Court of Human Rights accords a
"margin of appreciation" to nations with respect to some of the reasons
they might have for restricting protected rights. However, it has also
said that it expects that the margin of appreciation will narrow over
time – at least with respect to some rights – leading to the application

---

7 This line of argument was suggested to me by an oral comment by Rudolf Stichweh of the
University of Bonn.
8 For a discussion presenting the issues in more detail and with more nuance, see Whitman 2004.

of a European-wide rule in those areas. It might be thought that the idea of a narrowing margin of appreciation is analogous to the precipitation of rules out of a series of case-specific decisions. And, indeed, both processes do involve the passage of time and the accumulation of experience. But, the narrowing margin of appreciation results from what the European Court of Human Rights expects to be a normative convergence among European nations, not from some characteristic of experience with case-specific decisions. Put another way, given a specific and well-defined problem such as mandatory labeling of consumer products challenged as a violation of rights of free expression and self-realization, the European Court expects that over time an analysis of the regulation's proportionality will generate the same results in Germany, Latvia and Greece. But, this does not imply that the results with respect to that problem – nor with respect to any other – will be generated by a categorical rule.

Schauer's argument does bring to the surface an important question: It seems quite likely that rule-like approaches are normatively desirable with respect to *some* questions even if proportionality analysis prevails across a wide range. The clearest candidate for a rule-like approach is the law dealing with political speech critical of government policies. There are a host of institutional reasons – entirely apart from any theorizing about the foundations for a free speech principle – for placing sharp limits on a government's power to regulate such speech. For example, government officials are likely to be overly sensitive to such criticism and are likely to overestimate the harm that it does to admittedly important public interests such as stability and compliance with the law. Such regulations are often deployed in times of heightened political tension, which is likely to induce officials to be even more sensitive. The implication is that constitutional law must define the border between the domains in which proportionality analysis is appropriate and those in which a more rule-like approach is appropriate. Schauer suggests a historical account of the line-drawing process. Presumably one might devise a "meta-proportionality" analysis in which the line is drawn according to the principles of proportionality itself. But this is another area in which additional research would be valuable.

4.4   A different alternative to proportionality review

Proportionality review's structure is: Determination of infringement followed by an inquiry into whether the infringement is substantively justified. An alternative structure would replace the substantive inquiry with a procedural one: Was the infringing statute or regulation adopted through procedurally appropriate means? This inquiry has been called "due process of law-making" (Linde 1976), subconstitutional review (Coenen 2001) and semiprocedural review (Bar-Siman-Tov 2013).

In this form of review "appropriateness" refers to some judicially imposed procedural requirements beyond those required by the constitution for the adoption of the regulation at issue. Failure to comply with constitutionally required procedures invalidates legislation or regulations no matter what. If the constitution requires that electoral laws be enacted as organic laws by a qualified majority of two-thirds of the legislature, for example, such laws are invalid if the vote in favor is only 55 percent. An example of true subconstitutional review from the United States is *Hampton v. Mow Sun Wong* (1976).[9] There, the Civil Service Commission, the body charged with selecting and promoting government bureaucrats, had adopted a regulation barring all noncitizens from civil service positions, invoking concerns about foreign policy. The Supreme Court held that, although the Commission had been given authority by statute to make such a rule (which was therefore not *ultra vires* its *statutory* authority), the Commission was not the proper body for making such a decision; it had to be made by a decision-maker with direct responsibility for foreign policy. The decision did not foreclose the possibility of excluding noncitizens from the civil service and indeed, when the president imposed such an exclusion, the lower courts upheld it and the Supreme Court did not review those decisions.

The precise contours of subconstitutional review as a general phenomenon remain to be determined. Sometimes, as with *Hampton*, it involves a judicial decision to allocate decision-making responsibility among other institutions – there, from the civil service bureaucracy to the foreign policy one. Here the rationale appears to be expertise-related. Subconstitutional review allocates decisions to the institution best qualified to consider the relevant justifications for the infringement.

A similar form of institutional allocation might occur were the courts to require that some infringements be enacted through primary rather than secondary legislation. An example building upon a Dutch case

---

9 426 US 88 (1976).

is this: Twenty-four hour surveillance of those held in jails or prisons might not violate constitutional guarantees of privacy, but a court exercising subconstitutional review might hold that such surveillance can occur only when specifically authorized by the legislature and not through the general powers delegated to prison administrators. Here the rationale appears to be related to ideas about democratic fundamentals: Serious infringements, while constitutionally permissible, should have the support of democratic majorities expressed reasonably directly.[10]

The idea is captured by the *ultra vires* doctrine, which holds action by executive officials unlawful if the action is not authorized by primary legislation. As discussed in Chapter 2, it might also be used as the basis for interpreting constitutional provisions stating that limitations on constitutional rights must be "prescribed by law", with the word "law" here being interpreted to mean primary legislation.

Other examples of subconstitutional review involve judicial requirements that legislation or regulations be supported by reasonably detailed records (or, sometimes, finding the regulations constitutionally permissible in part because the records supporting them were sufficiently detailed). Here the rationale appears to be a judicial preference for seeing in the legislative process a kind of deliberative democracy.

This last example leads to consideration of some of the difficulties associated with subconstitutional review as it has been developed to this point. Constitutional courts do not and almost certainly could not, impose a requirement of a high degree of deliberation with respect to every statute or regulation. Subconstitutional review occurs with respect to some subset of all laws and regulations. The question then is: What is the proper domain of subconstitutional review? Because such review is triggered by the fact of an infringement, the domain cannot be the entire range of constitutional rights. Rather, the domain of subconstitutional review must be confined to a subset of rights. But which ones and on what basis can the courts specify them?

The structural similarity between subconstitutional review and proportionality review – with procedure replacing substance at the step of justification – suggests another question about subconstitutional

---

10 The decision of the Supreme Court of Israel dealing with coercive interrogation techniques has the structure of subconstitutional review and, if justified, might be justified on similar grounds.

review. Proportionality review has a reasonably well-defined structure. What would the structure of subconstitutional review be? Namely, is it possible to develop stages of the sort now embedded in proportionality review?

The identification of subconstitutional review as a distinctive form of constitutional review is relatively recent, although the practice may have deep roots. The questions about the domain and the structure of subconstitutional review are good subjects for future scholarly inquiry.[11]

4.5   The role of international law in domestic constitutional law

A wave of constitution-making and revision in the late twentieth century coincided with the rise of an international human rights regime. Integrating that regime and newer constitutions raises some important issues about the definition of rights when a domestic constitution incorporates international human rights norms.[12] Typically, constitutions treat international treaty obligations as hierarchically superior to national statutory law: A statute held by either a domestic or an international court to violate an international treaty obligation lacks domestic legal force. But what is the hierarchical relation between the international treaty obligation and the national constitution?

This question arises in a number of contexts. The simplest is one in which a treaty obligation is said to invalidate a provision of the national constitution. Without more, one obviously available response is to assert that the treaty, to the extent that it is properly interpreted, is inconsistent with the domestic constitution and was improperly entered into – that the nation's treaty-makers lacked authority under the constitution to accede to a treaty requiring modification of the nation's constitution.

---

11 Bar-Siman-Tov has offered a series of prescriptive rules that address the issues of domain and structure, the most intriguing of which is that subconstitutional review should be incorporated into proportionality review at the stage of "proportionality as such" (Bar-Siman-Tov 2013).

12 Some of the issues are traditional ones in international law – issues of compliance with international norms on the domestic and international planes, for example. The discussion here focuses on issues that have surfaced more recently.

More complicated are cases in which the nation's domestic constitution itself incorporates international norms in what is sometimes referred to as a "constitutional bloc", whether by referring to specific international human rights treaties, such as the Inter-American Convention on Human Rights, or by referring generally to international law. As a textual matter, the purely domestic constitution provisions are on the same plane as the international norms and one could rationally defend the competing propositions that the international norms supersede domestic constitutional provisions or that the domestic provisions prevail against the international norms. Here the precise wording of domestic constitutional provisions may matter a great deal.

Even more complicated is a subset of cases where international law has been incorporated into the domestic constitution. Suppose the relevant provision refers to the Inter-American Convention on Human Rights. That Convention is regularly interpreted by the Inter-American Court of Human Rights. Has the domestic constitution incorporated the jurisprudence of that Court, as it is articulated from time to time? Here too constitutional language may play an important role in suggesting the answer.

From the point of view of domestic constitutional law, the incorporation of decisions by transnational courts may be especially difficult. Consider first a constitution that includes an international treaty in the constitutional bloc, but expressly (or by interpretation) excludes the interpretations of that treaty by transnational tribunals. In the face of a claimed conflict between a constitutional provision and the treaty, the domestic constitutional court can develop its own interpretation of the treaty. That interpretation might be one that leaves the domestic constitutional provision untouched, or it might be one that invalidates the provision. In the latter case, however, the invalidation results from a *domestic* decision. The case is the same even if the transnational tribunal has offered an interpretation of the treaty provision different from the one the domestic court adopts, as long as the domestic court treats the transnational tribunal's interpretation as merely persuasive rather than authoritative.

The incorporation of decisions by transnational tribunals into the constitutional bloc may cause special difficulties. Transnational tribunals are structured so as to ensure some degree of responsiveness to the peculiarities of local conditions, through the guaranteed representation of a so-called "national judge" on the tribunal or through the inclusion on the tribunal of judges from every signatory nation. And, as the brief discussion of the "margin of appreciation" doctrine earlier suggests, transnational tribunals have developed doctrines that seek such responsiveness. Yet, we can be reasonably confident that neither the structural nor the doctrinal mechanisms will always ensure a "proper" degree of responsiveness. Or put another way, the transnational tribunal's decisions will sometimes fail to fit well into domestic circumstances and yet, their incorporation in the constitutional bloc makes them legally binding no matter what the domestic constitutional court might have done on its own. The Inter-American Court's decisions on the impermissibility of granting immunity for human rights violations to participants in a dictatorial regime, now replaced by a democratic one, might be an example: Continuing domestic support for representatives of the former regime may make immunity politically desirable and sometimes even essential, yet the Inter-American Court's jurisprudence makes it difficult for the new regime to offer immunity.

The difficulties associated with integrating international law and domestic constitutional law have only recently begun to emerge. Here too there are important opportunities for scholarly inquiry.

5 The structure of government

5.1 The classical enumeration of the branches of government and its modification

Generations of constitutional theorizing about the structure of government described all governments as consisting of three branches – the legislature, the executive and the judiciary. Each branch had distinctive functions, performed everywhere no matter whether the system was monarchical, parliamentary, or separation of powers. The legislature prescribed general rules, the executive implemented those rules and the judiciary resolved conflicts between private parties, or between the state and private parties, about the rules' application. The purveyors of early versions of the three-branch account understood that it concealed real complexities. Concerned in part about war-making, for example, John Locke identified a prerogative power in the executive to act against the law, as well as a federative power, also located in the executive, to engage in relations with other nations.

The idea that the sovereign was immune from challenge in "its" own courts posed another challenge: How could a system of government be designed that provided some assurance of fair treatment for complaints by individuals that executive officials had failed to comply with the rules set down by the legislature? Albert Venn Dicey summarized the tradition associated with common law systems in writing that any official "who exceeds the authority given him by the law . . . is amenable to the authority of the ordinary courts" (Dicey 1915: 389). By the time Dicey wrote in the late nineteenth century other national systems of government had adopted a different solution. Officials understood to be employed within the executive branch implemented the legislature's general rules, with the low-level officials who actually did much of the work understood as the recipients of power delegated to them by high-level executive officers. In civil law systems, citizen complaints about the actions of the low-level officials, which were handled in common law systems in the ordinary courts, were handled in special administrative courts.

Eventually, constitutional theorists reconceptualized the structure of government, adding a "fourth branch" to the classical three. The fourth branch consisted of the institutions of the modern administrative state, the bureaucracies that actually implemented the law and administrative tribunals. Acknowledging the existence of a fourth branch resolved problems that arose when theorists tried to fit the administrative state into the three-branch model.

Difficulties arose with respect to each of the three branches:

(1)   Legislatures enacted general rules, but those rules were often so general that implementing them required so much "fleshing out" with greater detail that it was unrealistic to describe what was occurring as the mere implementation of legislative rules. Realistically, the implementers were making law. The jargon of US administrative law captures the point in describing one large component of the action of the administrative state as rule-making. In the three-branch model, it appeared as if executive officials were exercising legislative power.

(2)   In the three-branch model the only plausible location for administrative tribunals was within the executive branch. Dicey and his successors in the common law world treated administrative tribunals as just another set of executive officials whose actions were freely reviewable in the ordinary courts. Elsewhere and as the administrative state matured in common law systems, that account was implausible. Adjudicators in administrative tribunals had – and had to have, if there was to be the minimal appearance of fairness – a degree of independence from supervision within the executive branch, which made it awkward to describe them as components of the executive branch.

(3)   Even describing the implementers of general law as executive officials came under some pressure. They gained protection against arbitrary hierarchical control as merit-based civil service systems developed. And particularly in US conceptualizations of the administrative state, the implementers drew upon specialized knowledge that required their insulation from policy-based pressure from their hierarchical superiors who were more responsive to ordinary political concerns.

The conceptualization of the modern state as having four rather than three branches became widely accepted in the twentieth century. Strikingly, though, that conceptualization was not widely reflected in constitutional documents, few of which give systematic attention to the institutions of the administrative state (Ginsburg 2010). Specific provisions do deal with aspects of the fourth branch, but they are rarely collected and organized in ways similar to the way constitutional documents treat the legislature and the executive branches. For obvious reasons, this sometimes provides grounds for constitutional controversies: How administrative bureaucracies are actually structured and what they actually do, do not map easily on to the three-branch model. When political circumstances are right, some will seize on the tension between the reality and the three-branch model to argue that something the administrative bureaucracy has done is unconstitutional.[1]

5.2   An emerging fifth branch of government?

By the end of the twentieth century gaps in the four-branch conceptualization began to appear. Systems of governance confronted a number of problems that can roughly be described as problems of conflicts of interest associated with the legislative and executive branches. The first institutions designed expressly to avoid such problems were probably central banks. They were charged with management of the monetary system. That task could not be performed well if their decisions were closely supervised by the political branches, as decisions by the administrative bureaucracy were because the decisions had to take a longer perspective than that taken by most politicians. Yet their decisions required the exercise of judgments on fundamental political questions that made complete independence from the political branches undesirable. And for most observers central bank decisions were not predicated on specialized technical knowledge in the way that many ordinary decisions by typical administrative bureaucracies were.

As the twentieth century progressed, other conflict-of-interest problems emerged. These included problems of corruption in the classic sense, disposition of electoral controversies and concealment of information. In traditional constitutional theory these problems were most extensively addressed by James Madison.[2] According to Madison,

---

1   In the United States, this is the basis for a controversy, beginning some time in the 1980s and extending to the present, over what is known as the "unitary executive" theory. Under that theory, all aspects of administration must be subject to ultimate control by the chief executive, a proposition that is incompatible with significant aspects of the way in which the US administrative state actually operates.

2   The Federalist No. 51 (Madison).

"ambition" could be set against ambition. That is, legislators would have an interest in identifying and publicizing corruption in the executive, and executives would have the same interest with respect to legislators. Legislators would seek information from an executive whose incentives were to conceal it and political forces would produce a resolution that revealed some information whilst keeping some concealed. Removed from ordinary politics, courts would solve election disputes. For Madison, then, the three-branch system provided the resources for dealing with conflict-of-interest problems by giving each branch an interest in identifying conflicts of interest arising in the other branches.

The Madisonian solution worked best in separation of powers systems, although norms of proper behavior might create similar, though probably weaker, incentives in parliamentary systems. The rise of organized political parties has rendered the Madisonian solution obsolete even in separation of powers systems (Levinson and Pildes 2006). Members of the executive branch and the legislature who are members of a single political party can be expected to support each other, at least in the absence of truly extraordinary circumstances. A president will protect corrupt legislators from his or her party from executive investigations (and, where the party holds a majority in the legislature, other party members will protect corrupt legislators from censure from within the legislature). Legislators will obstruct legislative investigations into the conduct of a president from their party. Some institutional mechanisms beyond the traditional three branches seem required to address conflict-of-interest problems adequately today.

Despite their seemingly disparate character, the conflict-of-interest problems share several general features: (1) They are problems *within* the executive and legislative branches. (2) For that reason, the institutions designed to deal with the problems would have to be independent of the legislative and executive branches, but – for reasons to be discussed – they should not be *too* independent of them. What was needed has been called a system of second-order accountability: accountability of institutions designed to ensure that other institutions are accountable. The three- or four-branch model already has institutions that are designed to be both independent and somewhat constrained by politics – the courts and especially the constitutional court. So, one might think that assigning the problems of corruption, district boundary definition and so on, to the courts would be sufficient. But (3) the resolution of these problems often has profound effects on the political system as a whole. Relying on the constitutional court to deal with them would thrust that court rather deeply into the kind of politics from which it ought to be substantially independent. Or, put another way, there is a desirable balance between independence and accountability in connection with constitutional interpretation and application. Assigning these conflict-of-interest problems to the constitutional court will shift that balance, probably in the direction of greater accountability. That new balance might be desirable with respect to the problems of corruption and the like but undesirable with respect to constitutional interpretation. (4) Finally, some aspects of the problems, especially those of corruption and dissemination of information, require for their appropriate solution the deployment of a kind of expertise that might not be found even in constitutional courts whose members are drawn not merely from the career judiciary but from the legal academy, legal practice and politics.

The emerging fifth branch of government includes institutions designed to deal with conflict-of-interest problems like these. According to one compilation, twenty states, most in the global South, have at least such institutions embedded in their constitutions (Ackerman, M. 2010: 272). Here we examine three problems of conflicts of interest – anti-corruption efforts, resolution of various election disputes and dissemination of information – each of which has slightly different characteristics. Examining them separately helps identify some of the general design issues.

A prefatory note: Many of the difficulties identified in the following paragraphs might seem to be resolved by assigning the tasks to existing courts, especially the constitutional court, rather than by creating separate institutions. After examining problems associated with creating separate institutions, the discussion will turn to problems associated with assigning the tasks to the courts.

5.2.1 Anti-corruption agencies

Suppose corruption is understood to be the violation of criminal law. Assigning anti-corruption efforts to the ordinary criminal process means assigning it to prosecutors. In many systems, however, prosecutors – particularly those dealing with high-level matters – are members of, or are closely controlled by, the executive branch. We can predict that anti-corruption efforts in the hands of politically responsive prosecutors will be used by the regime to punish its enemies and whitewash its allies and so experience has shown. In South Africa, for example, an elite unit within the national department of justice was charged with investigating allegations of corruption, and came under fire for selectively directing its attention to political opponents of Thabo Mbeki, the nation's president.[3] This effect occurs in part because, as discussed in the next paragraphs, the very definition of corruption is contestable and prosecutors can adopt definitions that disfavor the regime's opponents and favor the regime's supporters.

The natural response is to take anti-corruption prosecutions outside the ordinary system of prosecution, or to rely on elements of that ordinary system that are themselves strongly insulated from political control. Here another common design choice emerges. The anti-corruption effort can be done by the creation of a permanent anti-corruption agency, or on an ad hoc basis through "special prosecutors" appointed to examine a single incident, or through commissions of inquiry with similarly limited charges. Each of these designs is associated with problems that may lead to over-prosecution (or, in the case of commissions of inquiry, over-identification) of corruption.

The permanent anti-corruption agency faces two difficulties. One is that its staff will ordinarily try to justify its own existence by finding and exposing instances of corruption. We can predict that such an agency will over-identify corruption so that it can show the public that it is doing the public's work. Typically created in response to crises of confidence in government, those staffing the agencies may believe, often correctly, that ordinary people will be "hyper-sensitive to any sign that the agency is not strictly fulfilling its mandate ... " (Ackerman, M. 2010: 267). Finding "too much" corruption than there really is may occur because the definition of corruption can itself be a matter of real contention in many situations. Core examples of corruption are easy to identify: the exchange of cash to the personal use of a government official in exchange for a decision favorable to the person offering the cash. But, much "corruption" is subtler, easing toward ordinary patronage rewards – grants of contracts or official positions to arguably qualified political supporters, for example – and general favoritism in policy development to political supporters. We can expect that a permanent anti-corruption agency will tend to adopt generous definitions of corruption – that is, definitions that expand the agency's jurisdiction – for what are basically the reasons that every bureaucracy has for attempting to expand its jurisdiction.

---

3 *Glenister v. President of South Africa*, 2009 (1) SA 287 (CC).

Ad hoc agencies are subject to similar pressures. Reporting that an extended inquiry turned up no evidence of corruption is likely to lead to criticism of the special prosecutor or commission of inquiry for wasting the public's money. There is an additional problem associated with ad hoc agencies. Precisely because they are ad hoc, it may be difficult to define in advance the procedures for selecting them. Often there may be conventions that narrow the field. So, for example, in Great Britain commissions of inquiry are usually headed by judges. When the United States had a system of special investigators, they were chosen by a special "committee" of judges. These designs, however, do not insulate the ad hoc agencies from criticism as being "stacked" in their composition either for the government or against the government's targets.

This difficulty recurs in a slightly different form in connection with the ad hoc body's terms of reference. Whoever establishes the body – by definition some already established agency – must define its scope and faces problems no matter what: Make the terms of reference too narrow and run the risk of being charged with guaranteeing a whitewash; make them broader and run the risk that the ad hoc agency will range widely over the political system. The US system of special investigators was challenged at different times for precisely these reasons, the most notable one being the (politically motivated) claim that special investigator Kenneth Starr exceeded his mandate in pursuing charges that eventually led to President William Clinton's impeachment.[4]

What is required for good institutional design, then, is some system for selecting members of either permanent bodies or ad hoc commissions that guarantees them some degree of independence of the general political system, but not so much independence that they are insensitive to the political dimensions of their decisions, particularly about what to characterize as corruption.

5.2.2   Election disputes, including drawing district boundaries

Resolving election disputes is obviously politically contentious, in large part because the disputes typically arise after the event, such as after a close election. (Some election disputes arise before the elec-

---

4 In a related context, Jessie Blackbourn observes that so-called "independent monitors" and "independent reviewers" of anti-terrorism efforts in Australia and the United Kingdom "are . . . appointed by the government of the day" (Blackbourn 2014).

tion, as in cases where the qualifications of candidates are put in question, but even there the decision-maker knows the identity of the candidate and observers can evaluate the likely impact of the dispute's resolution on the election.) The dispute might be over a matter of fact, such as whether electoral fraud or intimidation affected the election's outcome (or where a potential candidate was born!). But, of course, participants in the dispute-resolution mechanism know or can make decent guesses about which side will benefit from determining those facts. The difficulties already mentioned of selecting members of ad hoc bodies recur.

For example, the US election of 1876 turned on determining whether electoral fraud affected the vote in three Southern states (and whether one elector from Oregon was eligible to serve). The dispute was resolved by an ad hoc body composed of fifteen members. At first, the plan was to have fourteen members on the Commission with obvious political affiliations, divided evenly between the parties and one independent member, David Davis, the only Supreme Court justice thought to be "above" party. Before the commission plan was adopted, however, Davis was elected to the Senate (as a Democrat) and resigned his seat on the Supreme Court. The commission then took shape. Five of its members were members of the US House of Representatives, five were Senators and five were Supreme Court justices. The party affiliations of every commission member, including the Supreme Court justices, were well known. There were two Democratic Senators and three Democratic Representatives, three were Republican Senators and two were Republican Representatives. With three "Republican" justices and two "Democratic" justices, the commission voted on strict party lines to award every one of the disputed votes to the Republican candidate – and this despite the fact that the evidence with respect to the different states was quite different in content and weight.

Problems of selecting members for ad hoc bodies can be reduced by choosing "truly" non-partisan members. But given the post-hoc nature of the problem, the incentives for those designing the institution and choosing its members all push in the direction of choosing members with real – if perhaps partially concealed – partisan leanings. Then, once the dispute is resolved, the losing side will inevitably seek out – and find, at least to their own satisfaction – indications that the crucial member or members of the institution were partisan from the beginning.

Having a permanent institution available to resolve election disputes might seem a promising alternative, because it would of necessity be created and staffed before any particular dispute arose. This design feature takes advantage of the benefits of a "veil of ignorance". Yet, because serious election disputes occur only when elections are close and because elections close enough for results to change when the institution resolves controverted questions of fact and law are rare, a permanent institution dedicated solely to resolving these disputes would often have little to do.

The solution to this problem is obvious: give the institution other tasks connected with the electoral process. For example, many election institutions are charged with resolving election disputes and setting district boundaries. One perhaps minor difficulty is that the expertise needed for drawing district boundaries is different from that needed to resolve election disputes and so, staffing the dual- or multi-purpose institution appropriately might be difficult. More serious perhaps is that the boundary-drawing process involves making ex ante choices – before an election – in a setting where sophisticated observers can make rather good guesses about the political consequences of one rather than another choice. In other words, boundary-drawing mixes an ex ante process with (quasi) ex post evaluations, and the ex post element introduces the same difficulties of selecting members for the institution that we have already seen.

Perhaps the most serious difficulty, however, is that the boundaries drawn must be in some general way acceptable to the political parties. Otherwise the boundary-drawing commission will be seen by some as simply a way in which partisans stack the deck in their favor.[5] Without some degree of support from political elites, the commission will find itself starved of resources. Some "deficit" might be made up by obtaining support from civil society – the press, social movements and NGOs. Yet, success probably depends on retaining significant support from the political parties that are themselves the source of the

---

5 One specific form of this difficulty deserves mention because it has occurred recently in the transformation of Hungarian constitutionalism in an authoritarian direction. The election-dispute and boundary-drawing body can be designed so that the party in power dominates its present composition, and the length of members' terms might be extended well beyond the present election cycle, thereby increasing the chance that the party presently in power will benefit from the body's decisions for the next – and perhaps more – election. Consider, for example, the creation of a body whose members serve for ten or fifteen years in a system that requires that elections be held at five-year intervals.

conflict-of-interest problem. As with defining corruption, the solution lies in ensuring that the commission's members have some degree of independence from the general political system, but not too much independence.

5.2.3   Dissemination of information

The design problems associated with dissemination of information are less serious. A permanent institution is rather clearly desirable with respect to "routine" information, though occasionally there might be a special need for an ad hoc institution to deal with revelation of particularly sensitive information, for example about national security. Still, decisions must be made about what types of information will be subject to disclosure. Some can readily be identified – information about the timeliness with which bureaucracies respond to applications and complaints, for example. But, most well-designed systems will have various exemptions – for information whose disclosure would improperly affect privacy or national security interests, for example. Constructing an institution that will deal with these exemptions sensibly may be difficult, for reasons already identified: An institution whose task is to disseminate information is likely to define its mission broadly and the exemptions narrowly. Here, too, recourse to courts seems attractive.

Yet courts have disadvantages associated with lack of specialization. Perhaps most important, sometimes information disclosure is effective only if done in a timely manner. If it takes years to find out that a bureaucracy takes three months more than necessary to process applications, for example, the information is unlikely to help any individual applicant, though it might prod the bureaucracy and its supervisors to redesign its processes. Courts might find it difficult to process requests for information disclosure promptly enough because they must also deal with ordinary criminal and civil cases.

5.2.4   Courts as an imperfect solution

Many constitutional systems use the courts as venues for dealing with these transparency issues. As discussed above, the institutions used to address corruption and election disputes must be both independent from the "political" branches and somewhat accountable to them. Courts and especially constitutional courts, have been designed with a combination of independence and accountability in mind (Lee 2011).

There are difficulties associated with using courts, however. These arise in connection with both ad hoc tribunals and the assignment of the tasks overall to some identified judicial body. Resolving these problems requires that the decision-makers combine legal and political sensitivity. To revert to the anti-corruption example: The decision-makers must develop a definition of corruption that is consistent with statutory and common-sense norms, but the definition must also be sensitive to the fact that much of what politicians do to gain support can be characterized as bordering on corruption. As Elliott (2013) puts it, "conduct can be evaluated . . . only with reference to particular standards or criteria: and the criteria . . . will inevitably be more diffuse, less objective and more contestable than those applicable to the determination of legal liability". The more judges, including constitutional court judges, are thought of as engaging in primarily legal tasks, with political sensitivity something of a disfavored component of the work, the less likely they are to combine legal and political sensitivity appropriately. They may, for example, focus primarily on the legal component of corruption's definition without taking its political context into account. Unlike ordinary courts, members of constitutional courts often – though not always – are chosen with concerns about the balance between independence and accountability in mind, so they might be thought suitable agencies for dealing with corruption and election disputes.

Further, constitutional courts are generalists in constitutional law. That means that they are less likely to become overly invested in defining corruption broadly than an agency dedicated to that task. It also means that they may find themselves at some disadvantage in dealing with the factual issues that arise in corruption and election dispute cases. And, more generally, their "mission" is enforcement of the constitution in general, not confined to the transparency issues discussed here.[6] That may help explain why constitution designers have often assigned transparency issues to the courts and especially to constitutional courts (Ginsburg and Elkins 2009).

---

6 Elliott provides a good summary of the difficulties in connection with ad hoc commissions and tribunals: "[A]ppointing a judge 'will not depoliticise an inherently controversial matter', such that judicial involvement in inquiries risks comprising perceptions of judicial independence; judges' capacity to handle legal and evidential issues in the courtroom may not be readily transferable to the inquiries context and may result in an unduly legalistic approach that renders the inquiry process almost impossibly unwieldy and expensive . . ." (Elliott 2013: 252).

Especially in contexts where the available pool of qualified people –
qualified in terms of legal and political sensitivity – is small, this solution might be sensible. Yet, it might sometimes become unsatisfactory
to the point of provoking constitutional crisis. The reason is simple.
The stakes in anti-corruption inquiries and election disputes can be
extremely high, with the control of the levers of government power
in issue. *Any* decision may provoke deep dissatisfaction among large
segments of the public and, perhaps more important, among political
elites. Experience around the world shows that these risks materialize
not infrequently. Perhaps we can say that the risks go with the territory, that is, they are built into the design and should be acceptable
for that reason alone. But there may be collateral effects on the constitutional court that perhaps should not be accepted with equanimity.
In particular, a court that is discredited among large segments of the
public because of its actions in an election dispute might find its cred-
ibility under fire in its ordinary work of constitutional interpretation.
What is needed, apparently, is to end up with a decent amount of
public acceptance (with the accompanying public disagreement) and
elite support.

These considerations suggest that constitution designers over the next
decades might take seriously the possibility of creating a "fifth" branch
of government – roughly, a transparency branch – different from the
judicial branch. The institutions within that branch might be loosely
modeled on the courts, particularly in seeking a combination of independence and accountability, but a combination probably different
from that sought in the judicial branch.

The difficult design issues are illustrated by the South African anti-corruption case mentioned above. South Africa has two constitutionally
rooted agencies dealing with crime: the National Prosecuting Authority
(NPA) and the South African Police Service. A statute enacted in 1998
created a Directorate of Special Operations, commonly known as the
Scorpions, within the NPA, to deal with what the Constitutional Court
described as "national priority crimes", especially organized crime and
corruption. The Scorpions' activities became politically controversial. Critics said that it engaged in selective investigation of President
Mbeki's political enemies. Supporters said that it was an extremely
effective anti-corruption unit, whose critics were themselves direct
or indirect beneficiaries of corruption. In 2007 the governing party's
national conference replaced President Mbeki as party leader with
Jacob Zuma. The conference also adopted a resolution committing

the party to dissolving the Scorpions unit. With Zuma now president, the Cabinet in 2009 introduced and parliament approved, legislation transferring the Scorpions' prior mandate to a unit within the Police Service (where it became known as the Hawks).

The issue before the Constitutional Court[7] was whether the replacement of the Scorpions with the Hawks violated the South African Constitution. Dividing five-to-four, the Court held that it did, because the Hawks lacked sufficient independence from political control. The reasons arose from the tenure provision for the Hawks' director and from excessive "political oversight". The majority's analysis of tenure is a bit obscure.[8] It began by observing that the members of the Hawks were "ordinary police officials" who did not take any special oath of office and later, observed that the Hawks "enjoy no specially entrenched employment security". The majority did not say why the ordinary official's obligation to enforce the law was different from the one imposed by an oath to enforce the law "without fear, favour or prejudice", but it did suggest that giving the Hawks ordinary employment security "is not calculated to instil confidence ... that they can carry out their investigations vigorously and fearlessly". For the majority, "the absence of specially secured employment may well disincline members of the Directorate from reporting undue interference in investigations for fear of retribution". This is so presumably because the high political stakes of their investigations would make their dismissal pursuant to ordinary disciplinary rules more likely than would be true for officials dealing with more ordinary matters. Further, the director of the Hawks was to be appointed by the Minister for Police "in concurrence with the Cabinet". The position was renewable, which "heightens the risk that the office-holder may be vulnerable to political and other pressures".

The majority's "gravest disquiet" came in connection with political oversight by a committee of Cabinet Ministers. That committee could issue guidelines, which "create[d] ... a plain risk of executive and political influence on investigations ... ". The guidelines might insulate offenses or "categories of political office-bearers from investigation". The majority conceded that that possibility "may be far-fetched", in part because the guidelines would have to be made public. More, though: The Ministerial Committee could engage in "hands-on super-

---

7 *Glenister v. President of the Republic of South Africa* [2011] ZACC 6.

8 Ibid., §§ 219, 222, 224, 228, 232, 234, 236, 243–5.

vision" through regular meetings and receipt of "performance and implementation reports".

The majority in the Scorpions case identified the core problem associated with anti-corruption efforts: "The competence vested in the Ministerial Committee to issue policy guidelines puts significant power in the hands of senior political executives . . . . [They] are given competence to determine the limits, outlines and contents" of the Hawks' work. According to the Court, that fatally compromised the endeavor. The majority acknowledged that "financial and political accountability of executive and administrative functions requires ultimate oversight by the executive". But, it concluded, the provisions at issue "go[] far farther than ultimate oversight [and] . . . lay[] the ground for an almost inevitable intrusion into the core function of the new entity by senior politics, when that intrusion is itself inimical to independence". The Court worried that "it is not unrealistic to conclude that the Ministerial Committee will be actively involved in overseeing the functioning" of the Hawks. "[S]ome measure of executive involvement" was appropriate, but under the statutes creating the Hawks, the extent of executive involvement "and the largeness with which its shadow looms in the absence of other safeguards" was "inimical" to independence. Parliamentary oversight, while welcome, was likely to be insufficient as one of those other safeguards.

Still, much of what the majority identified as compromises with independence are also mechanisms for ensuring accountability. The dissenters in the Scorpions case argued that independence was a "complex and context-specific" question and their reference to context might provide the answer to the issue of independence with accountability.[9] The provisions for oversight by a ministerial committee might be appropriate mechanisms for political oversight in some contexts, but perhaps not in South Africa, in light of the specific history that led to the demise of the Scorpions and the creation of the Hawks.

However the design issues are resolved, there remains the question of whether they should be statutory or constitutional. Institutions created by statute might fit awkwardly into the three- (or four-) branch model of government. A major US Supreme Court decision, for example, struggled over reconciling the statutory system of independent anti-corruption investigators, appointed by the courts, with the general

---

9 Ibid., § 114.

authority of the national executive branch to "take care that the laws be faithfully executed" through a purportedly exclusive control over prosecution.[10] The Supreme Court upheld the system, though many commentators believe that the dissent had the better of the constitutional argument.

At present these institutions are integrated into constitutions in several ways: ad hoc improvisation, usually in response to specific crises; informal grouping of the institutions in a constitution, with a great deal of common language dealing with independence and accountability; and the explicit creation of a fifth branch (Ackerman, M. 2010: 265–6). Yet, as Mark Ackerman (2010: 274) puts it, "the existing agencies normally fit uncomfortably into the existing constitutional framework". Precisely how to give constitutional status to both permanent and ad hoc institutions might be one of the tasks facing constitution designers in the twenty-first century.[11] "Older democracies would do well to learn from their younger cousins" (Ackerman, M. 2010: 266).

5.3   Beyond the fifth branch – or modifying the three-branch model

Drawing on some aspects of US experience, Roberto Mangabeira Unger proposed the creation of a "destabilization" branch of government (Unger 1987; see also Sabel and Simon 2004). Unger observed that all social institutions – government bureaucracies and agencies, but also private companies – eventually become ossified, adapting too slowly to changes in their environments. His destabilization branch would be authorized to intervene in such institutions to disrupt the routines into which they had settled.

As a general and utopian social theorist, Unger devoted little attention to the precise details of his proposal. He did not attempt to identify how the destabilization branch would be staffed, for example, nor how *it* would avoid the ossification he believed inevitable in other institutions. Nor has his idea been taken up in any serious way by constitution designers. Yet, we can get some purchase on the general idea if we return to the idea's origins in US judicial experience.

---

10 *Morrison v. Olsen*, 487 US 654 (1988).

11 Ackerman, B. 2000: 691–3, offers a sketch of an "integrity branch", though with little attention to design detail.

Unger's new branch reflected his thinking about what some US courts had done to reorganize numerous welfare state bureaucracies whose routine operation had, in the courts' view, led to violations of basic constitutional rights. These cases, which Abram Chayes labeled "public law litigation", were an outgrowth of the US judicial experience in attempting to eliminate racial segregation in US public schools (Chayes 1976). The story, in brief, is this: The US Supreme Court held unconstitutional such segregation. Politicians in the Southern states, the location of most formal racial segregation, resisted the Court's decision. Eventually the lower courts and then the Supreme Court, endorsed remedies for desegregation that required schools systems to adopt extensive programs of transportation of students to school, with the judges sometimes specifying the location of new school construction, or identifying academic programs that, the judges believed, would eliminate segregated conditions.

These desegregation decisions were sometimes controversial, but they led judges to believe that they could also intervene in other bureaucracies to protect constitutional rights. An extensive practice of prison litigation developed, for example, in which judges issued detailed orders prescribing the housing arrangements for prisoners, the range of temperatures to which they could be exposed and the organization of the provision of medical services to prisoners. Again, these decisions were controversial and the US Congress limited judicial intervention by statute. But again the decisions provided a model upon which other judges built in other areas such as provision of social welfare services.

The term "public law litigation" migrated to India, whose Supreme Court developed an extensive "public interest section" charged with bringing problems with the provision of social and economic rights to the Court's attention. Here, too, the Court's remedies aimed at disrupting the routine operations of ossified bureaucracies by forcing them to address persistent social and economic problems.

Today the idea that *courts* can "destabilize" bureaucracies in the service of constitutional rights is reasonably well accepted, although often the specific decisions courts make in destabilization litigation are politically quite controversial. An older tradition in thinking about institutional capacity suggests that courts are ill-suited to the destabilization task they have taken upon themselves, primarily because the way judges act in "destabilization" cases is in some tension with the way they act in more traditional cases, even those involving constitutional rights. Legal philosopher Lon Fuller argued that judicial efforts to address what he called "polycentric" problems were likely to lead judges to depart from judicial "proprieties" (Fuller 1978). Polycentric problems involve complex interactions among a large number of actors and interventions that deal with only one set of interactions – for example, those between prisoners and those providing them medical care – are likely to have unexpected and probably unanticipatable, effects on other interactions, for example, those between prison administrators and those who supply food services to the prisons. (Fuller described polycentric problems as resembling a spider's web, where a disruption at one node ripples through the entire web in unanticipated ways.) According to Fuller, judges who intervened in polycentric problems would find themselves tempted to try out tentative solutions, modify them based on experience, look outside the ordinary litigation structure for information and novel proposals and more – all things that, in his view, judges should not do (and probably could not do well). Fuller contrasted these polycentric problems with "bipolar" ones, such as those involving claims that an individual was wrongly convicted either because the statute authorizing the conviction was unconstitutional or because the procedures used in the trial failed to satisfy constitutional requirements.

The rise of public law litigation posed a challenge to Fuller's concerns about the judicial proprieties, because in public law litigation judges did indeed do everything that Fuller said they could not do (or ought not to do). Yet, court orders in public law litigation have regularly been more difficult to implement than orders in more traditional litigation, both for technical reasons – the judges may lack information about what interventions would be effective in specific bureaucracies – and for political reasons. The dialogic form of constitutional review discussed in Chapter 3 helps address the technical difficulties, because the back-and-forth of dialogue can provide the courts with information they might not have had at the outset. Whether the dialogic form effectively addresses the political difficulties remains an open question.

Fuller's essay on polycentricity was never fully worked out; he left it unpublished at the time of his death, although it had been circulated widely. The essay did not explain in detail why the iterative process of tentative solutions revised based on experience was inconsistent with judicial propriety. Future scholarship might do well to take up that question.

One possibility, suggested in some of Fuller's comments, is this: Experience with public law litigation has confirmed that judges in such cases will in fact do what Fuller thought they ought not to do. And, when a judge seeking to implement a constitutional right by intervening in an ossified bureaucracy first tries one thing, then another, the judge may end up redefining the underlying constitutional right, transforming it, as Fuller suggested, into a more tractable (and familiar) form. That is, the efforts made in public law litigation to ensure that bureaucracies protect or advance constitutional rights may lead to a transformation not in the bureaucracies but in the rights themselves. In US prison litigation, for example, challenges to overcrowded conditions as the infliction of constitutionally impermissible "cruel and unusual punishment" initially succeeded, but resistance to the decisions eventually led the courts to find constitutionally permissible conditions that at the outset they would have held unconstitutional. Even more, the definition of "cruel and unusual punishment" adopted to justify the judicial retreat in the face of resistance in overcrowding cases came to be applied in cases dealing with medical care and the environmental conditions of confinement such as temperature controls during summer and winter.

This possibility may be particularly worrying when interventions in bureaucracies deal with first-generation constitutional rights. Second- and third-generation rights are being given content today and it is neither surprising nor particularly troublesome that some basic aspects of those rights remain ill-defined. For example, we have not yet fully worked out the relation between the idea that there is a "minimum core" of social and economic rights and the idea that such rights can be provided "within available resources" pending their progressive development (to use standard formulations). If dialogic interactions produce one and then another definition of the underlying rights, we can understand the process as one in which judges are gaining insight into the content of the rights at issue.

But where we believe that judges have or should have a reasonably clear sense of what the rights' contents are, the process of definition and redefinition might well be troubling. The US prisoner rights' cases might be an example, to the extent that the constitutional right at issue there was a first-generation right against the infliction of cruel and unusual punishment. Even there, however, perhaps one could say that judges were learning about the right's content in a context that they had not previously dealt with.

Consider, however, the possibility of an intervention in a police agency aimed at ensuring that police officers do not violate core rights of free expression in connection with public demonstrations. Suppose, for example, that a court entertains a public interest action against a police department because it is persuaded that the instructions given to police officers about how to respond when a public gathering occurs have led to repeated violations of rights of assembly and free expression. The intervention might take the form of requiring the department to develop a program of education in constitutional rights for all its officers. The court would supervise the program's content to ensure that the officers were being given the correct information about the rights' content. But experience might show that police officers do not learn that content well. The dialogic interaction might lead the court to revise its requirements for the program's content – that is, to simplify what the officers had to be told about the rights of assembly and free expression. The danger with which Fuller is concerned is that the courts will then apply the simplified version of those rights in *all* the cases involving assembly they confront, not confining the version to the context of the educational program within the police department.

At present it is unclear whether, or the extent to which, Fuller's concerns about judicial improprieties have actually been realized in public law litigation, though there are some indications that some adverse effects on the substantive definition of rights have occurred in dialogic forms of public law litigation. Notably, we might be able to characterize Fuller as concerned with something like a conflict of interest internal to a judicial branch charged with the dual tasks of protecting constitutional rights in their classical form and protecting such rights against violations by ossified bureaucracies. Institutional conflicts of interest have led to the development of the fifth branch of government described earlier in this chapter. The possibility that similar conflicts of interest occur within the judiciary in connection with public law litigation suggests, at the least, that some serious thought should be given to the design of a destabilization branch separate from the judicial branch, even if the destabilization branch is given a more limited jurisdiction than Unger imagines.

5.4 Conclusion

The three-branch model of government served constitutionalists well for centuries. At some point in the twentieth century, however, its inconsistency with the actual form of modern governments became clear. Perhaps because the institutions of the administrative state grew incrementally, they have not been widely integrated into written constitutions as a "fourth" branch. The accumulation of experience suggests, however, that scholars of constitutional law could profitably devote attention to conceptualizing the actual institutions of the modern state in more complex ways, if only by proliferating the identification of its branches.

6   Conclusion

The study of comparative constitutional law has reached a mature stage. Some issues such as the basic justification of constitutional review exercised by independent courts in democratic societies have been explored in great detail. With respect to these issues new insights continue to be generated as experience reveals new facets of old issues and as small innovations in constitutional design raise unexpected new questions. More interestingly, perhaps, completely new issues continue to arise and provide opportunities for major advances in our understanding of constitutions and constitutionalism. This Conclusion addresses two of these issues.

Consider, for example, the emergence of a new generation of constitutionalized rights. Initially these new rights might appear to be a diverse group, encompassing rights of linguistic minorities, of indigenous peoples, of cultural minorities and rights, both of and in, the environment. Yet, understanding them leads us to examine some common themes. At the level of concrete implementation of these rights through institutional forms, each one requires that we identify someone or some group that is entitled – has standing – to assert the rights. Yet doing so almost inevitably fails to be fully responsive to important dynamic aspects of the underlying right or interest.

6.1   Forms of constitutionalism other than liberal constitutionalism

Undoubtedly because of their disciplinary commitments, legal scholars of comparative constitutional law typically assume that the object of their study is a normatively weighted one – liberal constitutionalism. Constitutions in authoritarian states are rarely examined, except as negative examples, because such constitutions do not serve simultaneously to allocate and limit the exercise of public power: Formal allocations of power in such constitutions may only accidentally correspond to the reality of power allocation and, by definition, public power in authoritarian states is formally unlimited.

Liberal constitutions are treated as a category of interest in two ways. Sometimes scholars posit an idealized liberal constitution and identify ways in which specific national constitutions fall short of realizing the ideal. These studies are basically exercises in political theory, with the major analytical work done in specifying the idealized liberal constitution. Studies of "shortfalls" deal with established and relatively stable constitutions. Alternatively, sometimes scholars describe constitutions in transition from something authoritarian or a shortfall to full liberal constitutionalism.

Probably motivated by scholarship in political science on "hybrid" or "semi-authoritarian" political systems, political scientists have recently turned their attention to constitutions and courts in authoritarian nations (Ginsburg and Moustafa 2008; Ginsburg and Simpser 2014; Moustafa 2007). As one summary puts it:

> Courts are used to (1) establish social control and sideline political opponents, (2) bolster a regime's claim to "legal" legitimacy, (3) strengthen administrative compliance within the state's own bureaucratic machinery and solve coordination problems among competing factions within the regime, (4) facilitate trade and investment and (5) implement controversial policies so as to allow political distance from core elements of the regime. (Ginsburg and Moustafa 2008: 4)

Constitutions organize power within a ruling authoritarian coalition and create mechanisms such as court review of administrative action that make it easier for the authoritarian rulers to gather accurate information about how policies adopted at the center are being implemented in the peripheries.

Legal scholars might profit from these efforts in political science, not merely because they offer interesting insights into how constitutions operate but also because they suggest the possibility of "pluralizing" the object of study in comparative constitutional law. Perhaps one can identify an "authoritarian constitutionalism", as might be suggested about Singapore (Tushnet, manuscript forthcoming). Pluralizing the object of study might also lead to a reconceptualization of the idea of "shortfalls". That is, some regimes that do not fit a posited ideal of liberal constitutionalism in some dimensions might be so stable that they deserve examination on their own terms. To offer a controversial example: The US Supreme Court has interpreted the national guarantee of freedom of expression to place sharp limits on the ability of legislatures to regulate expenditures on campaigns for election to office. Given the existing distribution of wealth in the United States, it might be that this interpretation in turn limits the effective ability of those who strongly dissent from the status quo distribution of wealth to have an effective voice in shaping public policy (Lindblom 1977). Few would dispute the proposition that the US constitutional system is not authoritarian and yet, if the status quo distribution of wealth is inconsistent with some liberal conceptions of equality the United States would not have a "truly" liberal constitution. Yet, the US system's endurance and seeming stability suggest that describing it merely as falling short of a posited liberal constitutionalist ideal will divert scholarship on to an unproductive path. It might be better to acknowledge the possibility of a plurality of constitutionalisms ranging from an idealized liberal constitutionalism to something short of pure authoritarianism.

6.2   Constitutions for modern and highly divided nations: contradictory definitions of "thin" constitutions

Historically nations could be united around ethnicity or a common heritage shared by all citizens. Ethno-nationalism is no longer available as a source of national unity in many nations today. Some nations are deeply divided internally. Some nations with a Muslim majority are divided between those who envision a constitution committed to secularism and those who envision one strongly influenced by Islam. Israel is divided between those who see the nation as primarily democratic and also Jewish and those who see it as primarily Jewish, understanding Judaism in strongly theological terms. Other nations have become nations of immigration, composed of citizens with generations of ties to the nation and citizens much more recently arrived.

Scholars of constitutional law have begun to examine whether and how constitutions can substitute for ethno-nationalism as a ground of national unity. The United States offers a model of sorts because its central commitments since its founding were constitutional, not ethno-nationalist. Yet, whether the US model is available in practice for other nations remains in question.

The text of the US Constitution is short. The texts of most modern constitutions are substantially longer. Simple comparisons of texts may not tell us much about constitutional law as a whole: An annotated US Constitution, with notes identifying US Supreme Court decisions interpreting each textual provision, could run to thousands of pages. But the comparisons of textual length may have some implications for popular understanding of specific constitutions.

An example is provided by discussions of a proposed constitution for Europe. The proposal was extremely long and complex, which became an independent ground of opposition to it. In some sense the length and complexity were intrinsic to the project – creating a governing structure for a multinational Europe. But, it was said, a constitution of that sort could not inspire the public and generate popular adherence to the constitution.

What could? Scholars and politicians have suggested that a "thin" constitution might do so, but they use the term "thin" in almost directly contradictory ways. For some, a thin constitution consists of fundamental propositions about the grounds of state power – typically, propositions associated with the liberal tradition. The rest of the constitution, they argue, consists of details whose purpose is to provide institutional means for implementing the thin constitution. A thin constitution of this sort, it is said, might provide the basis for national identity when ethno-nationalism is no longer available, as in nations of immigration and the imagined Europe unified under a constitution.

For others, a thin constitution consists of the details of government, with no commitments to fundamental values. Proponents of this view argue that some nations are so divided over fundamental values that the only path forward lies in putting in place a government that delivers social order and other basic goods and either deferring controversies over fundamental values to the future or relegating them to the ordinary politics that will occur within the framework created by this type of thin constitution.

6.2.1 The thin liberal constitution

In the course of the debate over the proposed constitution for Europe the German social theorist Jürgen Habermas (1996) articulated a position about constitutionalism that, he argued, was particularly suitable for modern conditions in which national populations were increasingly diverse and difficult to unify around ethnicity or appeal to historic traditions shared by all. According to Habermas, nations – and federations – could be sustained today only by what he called constitutional patriotism. The term referred to the acceptance – both rationally and emotionally – of broad liberal principles set out in an easily understood national constitution.

Complex modern constitutions could not be the objects of constitutional patriotism. Yet, as noted above, those constitutions are complex because they must be. They define the institutions used to develop public policy in many domains and variation among domains induces a corresponding variation among institutions: As described in Chapter 5, administrative agencies and transparency institutions must perform tasks once committed to legislatures. And, those agencies and institutions must fit together with each other and with the legislature and executive ministries dealing with similar problems.

Further, complexity has begun to affect the specification of broad liberal principles. Taking international human rights documents as a rough proxy for contemporary understandings of liberal principles, we can see that "liberty, equality and fraternity" or "life, liberty, property and the pursuit of happiness" are no longer adequate. The list of liberal principles now runs to several pages.

Does this imply that the quest for an understandable constitution should now be abandoned? That conclusion would be quite troubling. Much behavior dealing with constitutional norms occurs in ordinary political life. Voters choose among political programs that have constitutional underpinnings and implications. Legislators and executive officials develop and implement policies that also have constitutional underpinning and implications. As a practical matter much of this behavior escapes the view and control of specialists in constitutional law. So, the behavior will comport with constitutional norms only if ordinary citizens, legislators, bureaucrats and executive officials have some reasonable grasp of those norms. The constitution, in short, must be understandable to some important degree if we are to expect widespread compliance with its requirements. Further, if Habermas's analysis of modern social conditions is correct, the lack of an understandable constitution and the accompanying absence of constitutional patriotism might suggest that modern constitutions cannot significantly reduce the threat of disorder and instability associated with the deep ethnic, national, religious and other forms of pluralism found within today's nations.

One possibility lies in distinguishing between constitutional provisions setting out broad principles in one section (the "thin" part of the constitution) and provisions dealing with the details of government organization, the "thick" part (Tushnet 1999). Constitutional patriotism might be possible with respect to the thin constitution, which could be the object of organized programs of civic education, while only specialists would find the thick constitution a subject for serious attention.

Preambles and statements of principle might be vehicles for identifying what each nation regards as its thin constitution. Pursuing that course might require some revision in widespread views about the relation between constitutional review and preambles and statements of principle. The prevailing view is that preambles and statements of principles do not set out principles that constitutional courts will enforce against legislatures and executive officials. But, it seems unlikely that constitutional patriotism could be generated by unenforceable provisions, at least in nations – including most of those in the world today – where constitutional review in the courts is understood to be a basic feature of modern constitutionalism. An additional difficulty is that preambles and statements of principle might themselves become complex if they attempt to reproduce the entire range of rights regarded today as fundamental. Complexity defeats the project of constitutional patriotism and yet, paring down the list of fundamental rights might be politically impossible.

The project for a European constitution failed for many reasons. Its failure might suggest, however, that creating a thin constitution around which national identity can be formed today is more difficult than it was when the US Constitution was framed.

6.2.2   The thin purely institutional constitution

The thin constitution for Europe would have had liberal principles and little else. Proponents of the other form of thin constitutions imagine a quite different constitution, one with no principled commitments but only a detailed structure for organizing the government.

The thin purely institutional constitution is designed for what have been called deeply divided societies, where the divisions rest not so much on ethnicity and its analogues but rather on the very principles people seek to advance through politics. Division on such principles makes the other kind of thin constitution impossible. But, the argument goes, constitution-makers can put deep questions about principle to one side and design institutions that will allow a government to function in a reasonably effective way.

This kind of thin constitution cannot (and does not try to) transcend the deep divisions over principle. Instead, it commits choices with respect to those divisions to the political process that will be created under the purely procedural constitution. For political theorists that might be satisfactory because the institutions could be designed under what philosopher John Rawls called a "veil of ignorance". Such a veil makes it impossible for adherents of each competing vision of deep principles – secularists and Islamists alike – to know with confidence what policies will be adopted once the institutions begin to operate.

The difficulty, however, is that real world political processes do not take place under a veil of ignorance. The competing sides will examine purely procedural proposals with an eye to the results they expect will occur (Lerner 2012). For example, they will trace the likely membership of the constitutional court back through the nomination and appointment processes, to make guesses about the principled commitments likely to be held by those the judicial appointment commission (or president, or legislature) nominates for the court. Those guesses will be informed by experience with the ongoing political system. To continue the example, if a judicial appointment commission with substantial representation from the bar is proposed, people will know something about the ideological views likely to be held by the bar's representatives on the commission. Perhaps a purely institutional constitution might work were it to be adopted. But knowledge or even reasonably well-grounded predictions about what the institutions are likely to do once they are in place will impede the adoption of such a constitution in the first place.

Future scholarship might fruitfully develop both of these understandings of thin constitutions and the conditions under each might be created and sustained: How thin can the thin liberal constitution be? Can constitution-makers overcome the obstacles to implementing either the thin liberal or the thin procedural constitution that arise from the very conditions of deep national division they are designed to transform?

***

The topics briefly addressed in this Conclusion are only examples of issues in comparative constitutional law that have recently emerged on the scene. In no more than a few years additional issues will push forward. As a field of scholarly inquiry no less than as an arena of real political importance, comparative constitutional law is likely to remain a discipline deserving continuing attention.

References

Ackerman, Bruce (2000), "The New Separation of Powers" 113 *Harv. L. Rev.* 633.

Ackerman, Mark (2010), "Understanding Independent Accountability Agencies", in Susan Rose-Ackerman and Peter Lindseth (eds), *Comparative Administrative Law*, Northampton MA and Cheltenham UK: Edward Elgar.

Alexy, Robert (2002), *A Theory of Constitutional Rights*, New York NY: Oxford University Press.

Barak, Aharon (2012), *Proportionality: Constitutional Rights and Their Limitations*, Cambridge UK: Cambridge University Press.

Bar-Siman-Tov, Ittai (2013), "Semiprocedural Judicial Review" 6 *Legisprudence* 271.

Beatty, David (2004), *The Ultimate Rule of Law*, New York NY: Oxford University Press.

Bellamy, Richard (2007), *Political Constitutionalism: A Republican Defence of the Constitutionality of Democracy*, Cambridge UK: Cambridge University Press.

Berman, Mitchell (2010), "Constitutional Constructions and Constitutional Decision Rules: Thoughts on the Carving of Implementation Space" 27 *Constitutional Commentary* 39.

Black, Charles L. (1969), *Structure and Relationship in Constitutional Law*, Baton Rouge LA: Louisiana State University Press.

Blackbourn, Jessie (2014), "Independent Reviewers as Alternative: An Empirical Study from Australia and the UK", in Fergal F. Davis and Fiona de Londras (eds), *Critical Debates on Counter-Terrorist Judicial Review*, Cambridge UK: Cambridge University Press.

Bomhoff, Jacco (2013), *Balancing Constitutional Rights: The Origins and Meaning of Postwar Legal Discourse*, Cambridge UK: Cambridge University Press.

Calabresi, Guido and Philip Bobbitt (1978), *Tragic Choices*, New York NY: Norton.

Chayes, Abram (1976), "The Role of the Judge in Public Law Litigation" 89 *Harv. L. Rev.* 1281.

Cheibub, Jose Antonio (2007), *Presidentialism, Parliamentarism, and Democracy*, New York NY: Cambridge University Press.

Cho, Hong Sik and Ole W. Pedersen (2013), "Environmental Rights and Future Generations", in Mark Tushnet, Thomas Fleiner and Cheryl Saunders (eds), *Routledge Handbook of Constitutional Law*, London: Routledge.

Chryssogonos, Kostas and Costas Stratilatis (2012), "Limits of Electoral Equality and Political Representation" 8 *European Constitutional Law Review* 9.

Coenen, Dan (2001), "A Constitution of Collaboration: Protecting Fundamental Values with Second-Look Rules of Interbranch Dialogue" 42 *Wm. and Mary L. Rev.* 1575.

Dahl, Robert (1957), "Decision-Making in a Democracy: The Supreme Court as a National Policy-Maker" 6 *J. Pub. L.* 279.

Dicey, Albert Venn (1915), *Introduction to the Study of the Law of the Constitution* (8th edition), London: Macmillan & Co., Ltd.

Dixon, Rosalind (2008), "A Democratic Theory of Constitution Comparison" 56 *Am. J. Comp. L.* 947.

Dixon, Rosalind (manuscript forthcoming), "Constitutional Interpretation Curves".

Dixon, Rosalind and Tom Ginsburg (2011), "Deciding Not to Decide: Deferral in Constitutional Design" 9 *Int'l J. Con. L.* 636.

Elkins, Zachary, Tom Ginsburg and James Melton (2009), *The Endurance of National Constitutions*, New York NY: Cambridge University Press.

Elliott, Mark (2013), "Ombudsmen, Tribunals, Inquiries: Re-fashioning Accountability Beyond the Courts", in Nicholas Bamforth and Peter Leyland (eds) *Accountability in the Contemporary Constitution*, Oxford UK: Oxford University Press.

Elster, Jon (1995), "Force and Mechanisms in the Constitution-Making Process" 45 *Duke L. J.* 364.

Epp, Charles (1998), *The Rights Revolution: Lawyers, Activists, and Supreme Courts in Comparative Perspective*, Chicago IL: University Of Chicago Press.

Epstein, Richard (1995), *Simple Rules for a Complex World*, Cambridge MA: Harvard University Press.

Ewing, Keith, Tom Campbell and Adam Tomkins (eds) (2001), *The Legal Protection of Human Rights: Sceptical Essays*, Oxford UK: Oxford University Press.

Fontana, David (2011), "The Rise and Fall of Comparative Constitutional Law in the Postwar Era" 36 *Yale Journal of International Law* 1.

Fuller, Lon (1978), "The Forms and Limits of Adjudication" 92 *Harv. L. Rev.* 353.

Gardbaum, Stephen (2013), *The New Commonwealth Model of Constitutionalism: Theory and Practice*, Cambridge UK: Cambridge University Press.

Ginsburg, Tom (2010), "Written Constitutions and the Administrative State: On the Constitutional Character of Administrative Law", in Susan Rose-Ackerman and Peter Lindseth (eds), *Comparative Administrative Law*, Northampton MA and Cheltenham UK: Edward Elgar.

Ginsburg, Tom and Rosalind Dixon (eds) (2011a), *Comparative Constitutional Law*, Northampton MA and Cheltenham UK: Edward Elgar.

Ginsburg, Tom and Rosalind Dixon (eds) (2011b), "Deciding Not to Decide: Deferral in Constitutional Design" 9 *International Journal of Constitutional Law* 636.

Ginsburg, Tom and Zachary Elkins (2009), "Ancillary Powers of Constitutional Courts" 87 *Tex. L. Rev.* 1431.

Ginsburg, Tom and Tamir Moustafa (eds) (2008), *Rule By Law: The Politics of Courts in Authoritarian Regimes*, Cambridge UK: Cambridge University Press.

Ginsburg, Tom and Alberto Simpser (2014), *Constitutions in Authoritarian Regimes*, Cambridge UK: Cambridge University Press.

Graber, Mark (2007), "The New Fiction: *Dred Scott* and the Language of Judicial Authority" 82 *Chi.-Kent L. Rev.* 177.

Habermas, Jurgen (1996), *Between Facts and Norms: Contributions to a Discourse Theory of Law and Democracy*, Cambridge MA: MIT Press.

Harding, Andrew (2012), *The Constitution of Malaysia: A Contextual Analysis*, Oxford UK: Hart Publishing.

Hirschl, Ran (2004), *Towards Juristocracy: The Origins and Consequences of the New Constitutionalism*, Cambridge MA: Harvard University Press.

Hirschl, Ran (2005), "The Question of Case Selection in Comparative Constitutional Law" 53 *American Journal of Comparative Law* 125.

Hofstadter, Richard (1973), *The American Political Tradition and the Men Who Made It* (25th anniversary edition) New York NY: Knopf, p. 131.

Hogg, Peter and Allison Bushell (1997), "The *Charter* Dialogue Between Courts and Legislatures (Or Perhaps the *Charter of Rights* Isn't Such a Bad Thing After All)" 35 *Osgoode Hall L. J.* 75.

Holmes, Jr., Oliver Wendell (1897), "The Path of the Law" 10 *Harv. L. Rev.* 457.

Kahana, Tsvi (2013), "Majestic Constitutionalism – The Notwithstanding Mechanism in Israel", in Gideon Sapir, Daphne Barak-Erez and Aharon Barak (eds) *Israeli Constitutional Law in the Making*, Oxford UK: Hart Publishing, p. 73.

Kramer, Larry (2005), *The People Themselves: Popular Constitutionalism and Judicial Review*, New York NY: Oxford University Press.

Krishnaswamy, Sudhir (2009), *Democracy and Constitutionalism in India: A Study of the Basic Structure Doctrine*, New Delhi: Oxford University Press.

Landau, David (2012), "The Reality of Social Rights Enforcement" 53 *Harvard International Law Journal* 189.

Landau, David (2013), "Abusive Constitutionalism" 47 *UC Davis Law Review* 189.

Lee, H.P. (ed.) (2011), *Judiciaries in Comparative Perspective*, Cambridge UK: Cambridge University Press.

Lerner, Hanna (2012), "The Political Infeasibility of 'Thin' Constitutions: Lessons from 2003–2006 Israeli Constitutional Debates" 22 *J. Transnat'l L. and Pol'y* 85.

Levinson, Daryl (2011), "Parchment and Politics: The Positive Puzzle of Constitutional Commitment" 124 *Harvard Law Review* 657.

Levinson, Daryl and Richard Pildes (2006), "Separation of Parties, Not Powers" 119 *Harv. L. Rev.* 2311.

Lindblom, Charles E. (1977), *Politics and Markets: The World's Political-Economic Systems*, New York NY: Basic Books.

Linde, Hans (1976), "Due Process of Law-Making" 55 *Neb. L. Rev.* 197.

Mandel, Michael (1989), *The Charter of Rights and the Legalization of Politics in Canada*, Toronto: Wall & Thompson.

Moustafa, Tamir (2007), *The Struggle for Constitutional Power: Law, Politics, and Economic Development in Egypt*, Cambridge UK and New York NY: Cambridge University Press.

Note [Robert Nagel] (1972), "Legislative Purpose, Rationality, and Equal Protection" 82 *Yale L. J.* 123.

Nozick, Robert (1974), *Anarchy, State, and Utopia*, New York NY: Basic Books.

Persson, Torsten and Guido Tabellini (2003), *The Economic Effects of Constitutions*, Cambridge MA: The MIT Press.

Ronzai, Yaniv (2013), "Unconstitutional Constitutional Amendments – The Migration and Success of a Constitutional Idea" 61 *Am. J. Comparative L.* 657.

Rosenfeld, Michel and Andras Sájo (eds) (2012), *The Oxford Handbook of Comparative Constitutional Law*, New York NY: Oxford University Press.

Sabbagh, Daniel (2007), *Equality and Transparency: A Strategic Perspective on Affirmative Action in American Law*, New York NY: Palgrave Macmillan.

Sabel, Charles F. and William H. Simon (2004), "Destabilization Rights: How Public Law Litigation Succeeds" 117 *Harv. L. Rev.* 1015.

Sagoff, Mark (1974), "On Preserving the Natural Environment" 84 *Yale L. J.* 205.

Schauer, Frederick (2005), "Freedom of Expression Adjudication in Europe and America: A Case Study in Comparative Constitutional Architecture", in Georg Nolte (ed.), *European and U.S. Constitutionalism*, Cambridge UK: Cambridge University Press, p. 47.

Seidman, Louis Michael (2012), *On Constitutional Disobedience*, New York NY: Oxford University Press.

Sharlet, Robert (1993), "Chief Justice as Judicial Politician" 2 *East European Constitutional Court Review* 32.

Sikkink, Katherine and Margaret Keck (1998), *Activists Beyond Borders: Advocacy Networks in International Politics*, Ithaca NY: Cornell University Press.

Soichi, Koseki and Ray A. Moore (1997), *The Birth of Japan's Postwar Constitution*, Boulder CO: Westview Press.

Stephenson, Matt (2003), "'When the Devil Turns . . . ': The Political Foundations of Independent Judicial Review" 32 *J. Legal Stud.* 59.

Stone-Sweet, Alec and Kathleen Stranz (2012), "Rights Adjudication and Constitutional Pluralism in Germany and Europe" 19 *J. Eur. Public Pol'y* 92.

Tushnet, Mark (1999), *Taking the Constitution Away From the Courts*, Princeton NJ: Princeton University Press.

Tushnet, Mark (2007), *Out of Range: Why the Constitution Can't End the Battle Over Guns*, New York NY: Oxford University Press.

Tushnet, Mark (2008), "Some Skepticism About Normative Constitutional Advice" 49 *Wm. and Mary L. Rev.* 1473.

Tushnet, Mark (2009), *Weak Courts, Strong Rights: Judicial Review and Social Welfare Rights in Comparative Constitutional Law*, Princeton NJ: Princeton University Press.

Tushnet, Mark (2012), "National Identity as a Constitutional Issue: The Case of the Preamble to the Irish Constitution of 1937", in Eoin Carolan (ed.), *The Constitution of Ireland: Perspectives and Prospects*, Haywards Heath UK: Bloomsbury Publishing.

Tushnet, Mark (forthcoming), "Authoritarian Constitutionalism".

Tushnet, Mark, Thomas Fleiner and Cheryl Saunders (eds) (2012), *Routledge Handbook of Constitutional Law*, London UK: Routledge.

Unger, Roberto Mangabeira (1987), *False Necessity: Anti-Necessitarian Social Theory in the Service of Radical Democracy*, Cambridge UK: Cambridge University Press.

Weiler, Joseph H.H. (1995), "Does Europe Need a Constitution? Demos, Telos and the German Maastricht Decision" 1 *Eur. L. J.* 219.

Whitman, James. (2004), "The Two Western Cultures of Privacy: Dignity Versus Liberty" 113 *Yale L. J.* 1151.

Whittington, Keith (2009), "Judicial Review of Congress Before the Civil War" 97 *Geo. L. J.* 1257.

Widner, Jennifer and Xenophon Contiades (2012), "Constitution-Writing Processes", in Mark Tushnet, Thomas Fleiner and Cheryl Saunders (eds), *Routledge Handbook of Constitutional Law*, London: Routledge, p. 57.

Yap, Po Jen (2013), "Dialogue and Subconstitutional Doctrines in Common Law Asia" *Public Law* 779.

Zoller, Elisabeth (2010), "Laïcité in Comparative Perspective: Panel Discussion" 49 *J. Catholic Leg. Stud.* 101.

Index

abusive constitutionalism 12
Ackerman, Bruce 108
Ackerman, Mark 98–9, 108
ad hoc commissions 104
administrative bureaucracies 96
adoption of constitution, inclusiveness
        22–4
affirmative action programs 82–3
Alexy, Robert 75, 84–5
alternative transferable vote 3
amendments, constitutional
    the doctrine of substantive
            unconstitutionality 30–32
    versus replacement constitutions 6–7,
            11–12
ancien regime 16, 18
anti-corruption agencies 98–100
Articles of Confederation, US 13, 15–16
Australian Constitution 27
authority, constitution's claim to 15

balancing, comparison with
        proportionality and rules 71–83
    generalized balancing 74
    high-low categories 76
    institutional risk of error analysis
            79–81
    objectivity 74–6, 80
    rule plus numerous exceptions
            structure 77, 86
    simplicity 77–81
    transparency 81–3
bankruptcy laws 33–4
Bar-Siman-Tov, Ittai 89, 91
Basic Law, Germany 16–17
    eternity clause 28
Berman, Mitchell 77–8

Black, Charles 27
Blackbourn, Jessie 100
Bobbitt, Philip 81
boundary-drawing, limits on rights 84–5
branches of government
    classical enumeration and modification
            94–6
    emerging fifth branch 96–108
    fourth branch, adding 95–6
    modifying three-branch model 108–13
    Montesquieu on 3
Bushell, Allison 57
by law clauses 34

Calabresi, Guido 81
Canada
    Charter of Rights and Freedoms 7,
            57, 84
    whereas clause preceding 26
    override mechanism 57
    Supreme Court 57
categorical analysis, and proportionality
        84
Central and Eastern Europe,
        constitutional negotiations 17
Chayes, Abram 109
Chinese Communist Party 63
Cho, Hong Sik 68
Chryssogonos, Kostas 3
citizen actions 54
citizen complaints 94
Civil Service Commission, US 89
Clinton, William (Bill) 100
coalitions/coalition bargaining 60, 62
Coenen, Dan 89
coercive orders, first-generation rights
        63–4

Colombia, Constitutional Court 30
commissions of inquiry, UK 100
Communist parties, Central and Eastern
    Europe 17
comparative politics 4
computerization 6
concretization, of abstractly described
    constitutional terms 58
conflicts
    conflict-of-interest problems 96–8
    constitutional 49–50
    intra-group 68
constituent power 13–19, 29
constitutional bloc 92
constitutional law, versus liberal
    constitutionalism 12–13
constitutional review 6, 42, 49
    battle of the courts 52–3
    coalitions/coalition bargaining 60, 62
    Commonwealth model 57
    countermajoritarian difficulty,
        constitutional theory 56–9, 61,
        65
    decisions
        *Government of South Africa v.
            Grootboom* (2000) 66
        Marbury v. Madison (1803) 42
        *President of the Republic of South
            Africa v. Hugo* (1997) 43
    dialogic 57–61
    dominant-party systems 62
    establishing 41–4
    human rights violations 51
    individual-level and systemic remedies
        65–6
    insurance models 41
    judicial selection 49
    justiciability doctrines 53–5
    Kelsenian model (centralized system)
        48–55
    one and done strategy 42–3
    political constitutionalism as
        alternative to 44–8
    political questions doctrine, US 54–5
    semiprocedural review 89
    and standing 48, 54
    statute, outdated 59–60

statutory interpretation 49, 52
structures 40–69
    classical issues 48–56
    first-generation (classical) rights 63–4,
        111
    government structure issues 51
    new 56–63
    second-generation rights 64–6
    third-generation rights 67–9
    and subconstitutional review 62–3,
        89–91
    unconstitutional details 59–60
    US model 48, 50–51, 53, 55
    weak-form 57
constitutionalism
    forms 114–16
    hybrid or semiauthoritarian systems
        115
    shortfalls 115–16
constitution-making 10–39
    backward- and forward-looking
        statements 25, 27
    best practice 23
    crowd-sourcing 19–24
    decisions
        *Australian Capital Television v.
            Commonwealth* (1992) 27
        McCulloch v. Maryland (1819) 36
        Olga Tellis v. Bombay Municipal Corp
            (1985) 28
        State v. Makwanyane (1995) 32
    deferring issues for further resolution
        32–6
    federalism 30, 33
    foundation (constituent power) 13–19,
        29
    foundational principles, expressing
        25–8
    inclusiveness 19–24
    post-conflict versus discredited system
        12
    processes 19–24
    ratification processes 22–4
    reasons for 10–13
    scope and comprehensiveness 24–36
    substance 24–36
    unamendability 28–32

constitutions
compliance with 36–8
foundational principles, expressing
25–8
making *see* constitution-making
preambles 25–6
thick 119
thin, contradictory definitions 116–21
cosmopolitanism 8
countermajoritarian difficulty,
constitutional theory 56–9, 61, 65
courts
battle of (conflict between
constitutional courts and
ordinary courts) 52–3
diffuse support for 31
as imperfect solution 103–8
political constitutionalism as
alternative to constitutional
review in 44–8
transnational 55–6
see also constitutional review
crowd-sourcing 19–24

Dahl, Robert 61–2
data bases 6–7
Davis, David 101
decolonization, twentieth century 16, 51
decree-laws 40
defamation law 87
deferral of issues 32–6
delegated legislation 40
demos (people) 13–14
destabilization of bureaucracies 109–10
detention, pre-trial 35
dialogic review 57–61
Dicey, Albert Venn 94
dictatorships, displacement (1970s) 1
dispensing power 53
distributive justice 13
Dixon, Rosalind 7, 32–6, 59
domestic constitutional law, role of
international law in 4–5, 91–3
drafting of constitutions
inclusiveness 19–22
openness 21–2
roundtable negotiations 17

elections
disputes 100–103
systems 4, 33
Elkins, Zachary 6
Elliott, Mark 104
Elster, Jon 18–19, 21
environmental rights 68–9
Epstein, Richard 77
equality 30, 32
electoral 3
violations, remedy for 64
European Convention on Human Rights 5
European Court of Human Rights 55,
87–8
European Court of Justice 55
extensional equivalence 73

false necessity problem 8
federalism 30, 33, 48
first-generation rights, constitutional
review structure 63–4, 111
first-past-the-post plurality rules 3, 33
Fontana, David 1
foreign affairs, political questions
doctrine 55
foundational principles, expressing 25–8
France
French Constitution 24
French Constitutional Council 27
French Revolution 13
religious clothing, limiting 51
freedom of expression, US law 77–8,
82–3, 86
Fuller, Lon 110–12

Gardbaum, Stephen 57
Germany
Basic Law 16–17
"eternity" clause 28
Federal Constitutional Court 5–6
Ginsburg, Tom 6–7, 32–4, 63, 96, 115
God, supremacy of 26–7
government structure 94–113
anti-corruption agencies 98–100
branches
classical enumeration and modification
94–6

emerging fifth branch 96–108
fourth branch, adding 95–6
modifying three-branch model 108–13
Montesquieu on 3
courts, as imperfect solution 103–8
decisions
    Glenister v. President of South Africa
        (2011) 99, 106
    Morrison v. Olsen (1988) 108
destabilization of bureaucracies 109–10
dissemination of information 103
election disputes 100–103

Habermas, Jürgen 117–18
harmonization 2–3
hate speech regulation 70
Hawks (Police Directorate for Priority
    Crime Investigation, South Africa)
    106–7
Herder, Johann Gottfried von 2
Hitler, Adolf 12
Hofstadter, Richard 36
Hogg, Peter 57
Holmes, Oliver Wendell 38
human rights violations, constitutional
    review 51
Hungarian Constitution 25, 102

Icelandic constitution 19–20, 24
inadmissibility 29
inclusiveness, constitution-making
    in adoption 22–4
    in drafting 19–22
    inconsistency in suggestions 20
independent monitors 100
India
    Constitution 27–8
    judiciary 62
    Supreme Court 28, 109
indigenous cultures, third-generation
    right to intellectual property 67–8
information, dissemination of 103
infringement, proportionality analysis
    72–3, 88–9
"institutional risk of error" analysis 79–81
insurance models of constitutional review
    41

Inter-American Convention on Human
    Rights 5, 92
Inter-American Court of Human Rights
    5, 55, 92–3
International Association of
    Constitutional Law 1
*International Journal of Constitutional
    Law* 1
international law, role in domestic
    constitutional law 4–5, 91–3
Iraq, Constitution of 26
Irish Constitution 25–8
Israel
    constitutional history 60
    election of prime minister experiment
        20
    parliamentary supremacy 41
    Supreme Court 6, 90

judicial balancing ("all things considered"
    approach) 82
judicial constitutionalism 47
judicial review 6, 40
justiciability doctrines, constitutional
    review 53–5

Kahana, Tsvi 32, 36
Kelsen, Hans (constitutional review
    model) 48–55

language 5–6
large-N-studies 6–8
leaking of information 21
Lee, H.P. 103
legislation vetting agencies 47
Levinson, Daryl 52
liberal constitutionalism 8, 12–13
Lincoln, Abraham 36
Linde, Hans 89
Locke, John 94

Madison, James 96–7
majestic constitution 36
Malaysia, Federation of 13
Mandela, Nelson 43
margin of appreciation 88
Marshall, John 36

Mbeki, Thabo 99, 105
Melton, James 6
minimal rationality requirements 73
Montesquieu, Charles-Louis de Secondat
    2–5, 8
Montevideo Convention on Rights and
    Duties of States (1933) 10
Moustafa, Tamir 63, 115

National Party, South Africa 17
national priority crimes 105
National Prosecuting Authority (NPA),
    South Africa 105
national security, political questions
    doctrine 55
national sovereignty 2
nations
    of immigration 26
    modern and highly divided 116–21
    spirit of 2, 8
negative power, constitutional review
    50–51
New Zealand 41, 58
non-governmental organizations (NGOs)
    14, 19, 68
Nozick, Robert 13

objectivity 74–6, 80
    rights analysis 74–6, 80
one and done strategy, constitutional
    review 42–3
openness, in drafting 21–2
organic laws 33

parliamentary supremacy 41, 44
path-dependency 84
Pedersen, Ole W 68
Pildes, Richard 52
political constitutionalism
    as alternative to constitutional review
        44–8
    constitutional conscientiousness 45–7
    fox-and-chicken-coop question 45
    party competition 45–6
    views of constituents 45–6
political questions doctrine, US 54–5
polycentricity 110

popular constitutionalism 44
post-communist constitutions 18
power
    constituent 13–19
    constitutions as maps of 11
    dispensing 53
    executive 34
    negative 50–51
    prerogative 53–4, 94
preambles 25–6, 119
prerogative power 53–4, 94
privative clauses, British constitutional
    theory 54
proportional representation (PR) 3, 33
proportionality analysis 1–2
    and categorical analysis 84
    comparison of balancing and rules
        with proportionality 71–83
    generalized balancing 74
    high-low categories 76
    institutional risk of error analysis
        79–81
    objectivity 74–6, 80
    rule plus numerous exceptions
        structure 77, 86
    simplicity 77–81
    transparency 81–3
    infringement 72–3, 88–9
    meta-proportionality analysis 88
    review structure, alternative to 88–91
public interest actions 54
public international law 4

ratification processes, constitution-
    making 22–4
reasonableness review 55
reciprocity principle 35
replacement constitutions, versus
    amendments 6–7, 11–12
review, constitutional see constitutional
    review
rights analysis 70–93
    boundary-drawing, limits on rights
        84–5
    comparison of balancing,
        proportionality and rules 71–83
    decisions

Hampton v. Mow Sun Wong (1976) 89
United States v. Stevens (2010) 78
differences in national substantive
    doctrines 83–8
environmental rights 68–9
first-generation rights, constitutional
    review structure 63–4, 111
individual-level and systemic remedies
    65–6
internal and external limits on 84–5
international law, role in domestic
    constitutional law 91–3
policy and rights, independent
    judgments 75–6
right-to-medication cases, South
    America 65–6
second-generation rights,
    constitutional review structure
    63–6
third-generation rights, constitutional
    review structure 67–9
see also proportionality
romantic nationalism 2
roundtable negotiations, constitution
    drafting 17
Russia, Constitutional Court 43

Sabbagh, Daniel 82–3
Sagoff, Mark 69
Schauer, Frederick 84–5, 87–8
Scorpions (Directorate of Special
    Operations, South Africa) 105–7
second-generation rights, constitutional
    review structure 63–6
secularism 30
semiauthoritarian political systems 115
semiprocedural review 89
sensitivity, political 50, 55
sexually explicit material,
    constitutionality of ban on 83
"sham" constitutions 11
Sieyès, Abbé 24
simplicity, rights analysis 77–81
Simpser, Alberto 115
South Africa
    anti-corruption agencies 98–9,
        104–7

Constitution 4–5, 17–18, 25, 32, 34–6,
    106
Constitutional Court 106
constitutional review 43
Ministerial Committee 106–7
Police Service 105
sovereign immunity 94
Soviet Union, breakdown 1
Stalin Constitution (1936), Soviet Union
    11
standing, and constitutional review 48, 54
Starr, Kenneth 100
statutes
    challenging as unconstitutional 72
    interpretation 49, 52
    outdated 59–60
    reading up and down 64
Stephenson, Scott 60
Stichweh, Rudolf 87
Stone-Sweet, Alec 53
Stranz, Kathleen 53
Stratilatis, Costas 3
subconstitutional review 62–3, 89–91
substance, constitution-making 24–36
    foundational principles, expressing
        25–8
    unamendability 28–32
substantive unconstitutionality doctrine
    30–32

thin constitutions
    contradictory definitions 116–21
    liberal 117–19
    purely institutional 119–21
third-generation rights, constitutional
    review structure 67–9
transitional constitutions 17
transnational courts 55–6
transparency, rights analysis 81–3
tribunals, transnational 92–3
Tushnet, Mark 57, 70, 119

ultra vires (beyond power doctrine) 40,
    52, 89–90
unamendability 28–32
unconstitutional amendments doctrine
    30–31

Unger, Roberto Mangabeira 108
unitary executive theory, US 96
United Kingdom
    commissions of inquiry 100
    Human Rights Act 1998 5, 44, 58
    parliamentary supremacy 41
    privative clauses, British constitutional
        theory 54
    secondary legislation 40
United States
    administrative rules/administrative
        state 40, 95
    Articles of Confederation 13, 15–16
    constitutional review model 48, 50–51,
        53, 55
    constitutional system 7, 34, 116–17
    Declaration of Independence 29
    federalism 30, 33, 48
    freedom of expression 77–8, 82–3, 86
    hate speech 70
    political constitutionalism 45–6

    political questions doctrine 54–5
    standing doctrine 54
    Supreme Court 45, 61, 78, 84, 87, 89,
        107–8, 116
    unitary executive theory 96
units of comparison 6
Universal Covenant of Human Rights
    84
Universal Declaration of Human Rights
    57–8
Uribe, Alvaro (president of Colombia)
    30–31

West Germany, Basic Law 16–17
    eternity clause 28
Whitman, James 87

Yap, Po Jen 63

Zoller, Elisabeth 70
Zuma, Jacob 105–6